HEROES
OF A
SPECIAL KIND

A Tribute to Special Olympics—
Its Coaches and Volunteers

Mary Francess Froese

Evergreen Communications, Inc.
Ventura, California

Heroes of a Special Kind

Published by
Evergreen Communications, Inc.
2085-A Sperry Avenue
Ventura, California 93003
(805) 650-9248

Scripture quotation used on the dedication page is taken from the King James Version (KJV) of the Bible. Public domain.

Library of Congress Cataloging-in-Publication Data

Froese, Mary Francess, 1941–
    Heroes of a special kind / Mary Francess Froese.
    p. cm.
    Summary: Profiles fourteen Special Olympics coaches and describes the work they do in the United States and Australia.

    ISBN 0-926284-15-0 : $12.95

    1. Coaches (Athletics)—United States—Australia—Biography—Juvenile literature. 2. Special Olympics—Juvenile literature. [1. Coaches (Athletics) 2. Special Olympics.] I. Title.
    GV696.A1F74 1991
    796'.092'2—dc20
    [B]   91-7192
                     CIP
                     AC

99 98 97 96 95 94 93 92 91 9 8 7 6 5 4 3 2 1

Printed in the United States of America.

To

Joel,
my son,
my inspiration.

Behold, I send my angel before you
to keep you in the way and lead you
in the path that I have prepared for you.
Exodus 23:20, KJV

The Special Olympics Oath

Let me win,
but if I cannot win,
let me be brave in the attempt.

Foreword

Heroes Of A Special Kind is a most fitting title for a book about Special Olympics volunteers. If there's a single reason why Special Olympics has had such remarkable growth in every state and nearly 100 countries of the world, it is the dedication, the skills, and the devotion of the more than 500,000 volunteers.

Who are these volunteers, these "special heroes"? They are parents, teachers, students, coaches, businessmen, and businesswomen. Many volunteers have come from the ranks of Special Olympics itself. They are the heart and soul of a grass-roots program that depends on volunteers to do almost every job needed to run a year-round program, from coaching athletes to raising money, from providing transportation to serving meals and handling public relations.

The heroes described in this book are people who would deny that they are heroes if you ask them. They would say that they are just ordinary people who have found in Special Olympics not only a chance to help others, but to learn and grow themselves. Special Olympics lets them share with the athletes and their fellow volunteers the true meaning of sports, skills, courage, sharing, and joy.

Eunice Kennedy Shriver
Founder
Special Olympics International

Waiting Arms

Excitement and expectation tighten around the group of people crowded into the airport waiting room. Shadows of early evening crawl across the runway as first one eager face and then another peers out the window at the approaching aircraft.

Finally from within the crowd comes the shout, "They've landed!" As parents and friends, we line the arrival aisle, awaiting our athletes, athletes of a special kind.

The doors swing open. Cheers and clapping explode all around as the young, and not-so-young, athletes emerge. Calls of greeting become exuberant roars as the athletes are reunited with loved ones amid hugging, backslapping, and excited laughter.

The athletes are Special Olympians, people who are mentally and physically disabled, ranging in age from 8 to 65. They have spent the past three days competing in their special events at the Berkeley campus of the University of California.

The first athlete to deplane is a young woman who appears to be in her late teens. Her dark, curly hair is rumpled from the plane ride; her Special Olympics sweat suit has the same rumpled look. The past three days of intense activity are reflected in the fatigue in her eyes. About four-feet-eleven, she is a little on the chubby side. One hand is drawn up and held limply against her body. She walks with a sliding gait. As she sees the crowd, her good hand immediately reaches to the medal hanging around her neck and her face lights up with an enormous smile.

Next comes a man who looks forty-ish; his ebony face etched with the beginnings of a beard. His bulging muscles hint that he's a power-lifter. The only outward indications of retardation are the Special Olympics sweatshirt he proudly wears and the medal hanging around his neck—a gold one. His infectious smile portrays innocence, one of the gifts granted those with mental retardation. His personal cheering section approaches him and he is enveloped in bear hugs.

Bystanders are visibly touched and can be seen smiling warmly and dabbing at moist eyes as they observe the returning athletes basking in their importance.

Once the athletes are safely off the plane, the Special Olympics volunteers disembark—businessmen, teachers, nurses, handymen, truck drivers, students—people from all walks of life. They spend hours, days, and weekends struggling to teach simple skills such as dribbling a basketball, pushing a puck, or throwing a disk; oftentimes the learning is at an agonizingly sluggish pace. The volunteers look spent but gratified as they observe the heroes' welcome their athletes are receiving.

I spot my son Joel's lanky six-foot frame and have eyes for no one else. He sees me and lopes toward our group. He shuffles his feet, forever dragging the toe of his left foot.

His right hand, twisting uncontrollably in his excitement, waves in the air. His face is alight with a proud grin as he bellows, "Hi, Mom, see me!" His dad and his care provider, Cathy, and other friends, gather round to exclaim over his medal. I corner Joel's coach and through a huge lump in my throat try to express my gratitude for his help and interest in my son. We laugh, and Joel blushes as the coach exclaims, "Joel tried to bring home every phone book in Oakland! He was pretty indignant when I wouldn't let him keep them."

The crowd slowly disperses. I put my arm through Joel's and, as we walk along, a feeling of pure joy envelopes me.

I watch other volunteers turn their charges back to the protection of parents or guardians before walking away. I realize I don't even know the name of the middle-aged man who worked with and cared for my son these past three days. Joel says his name is Bob.

I whisper to myself, "Many thanks, Bob! You're a hero of a special kind!"

Mary Francess Froese

Acknowledgments

I am deeply grateful to the many people who are responsible for the finalization of this book. Above all, thanks go to my heavenly Father for His inspiration and guidance. He almost made it a write-by-number project, for He laid the whole project out before me and implanted thoughts and ideas into my head that I had no trouble admitting were not mine, but His.

To Allen, my husband and chief photographer;

To Bob and Cathy Jardine, who have lovingly cared for my Joel these past ten years;

Then the many friends who helped birth the book by their prayers:

- —My Sunday School class at North Vista Baptist Church;
- —My Tuesday evening prayer group: Rita Walters, Barbara Scudder, and Denise Shaver;
- —My friends at the Vista Courthouse Bible Study;
- —Annie Carter, my spiritual mentor;
- —Doris Poole, Betty Stuart, Elaine Stillman,

Marylyn Murray, Ocull Pollard, Jean Ann Mayberry, Lenore Averell, Fran Schaad, Marie Coleman, Pat Savas, Scott Froese, and his church family at Neches First Baptist Church, Neches, Texas; and to

—Julie Pendray Steiner and Gloria Valencia Cothran, friends who patiently and lovingly edited my work.

And special thanks to:

—The State Special Olympics officials who nominated the special heroes for the book: Debbie Martin, Missouri; Melissa Weeks, Mississippi; Barb Mosher, Michigan; Chris Hahn, Oklahoma; Mickey Boutilier, Maine; Nancy Bottelo, Hawaii; Ronnie Floyd, Alabama; Robyn Cook, Australia;

—Herb Kramer, Special Assistant to Mrs. Shriver, who has been helpful in so many ways; and

—Paul Klein, Area Director, North San Diego County.

Blessed Are You

Blessed are you who take time to listen to difficult speech, for you help us to know that if we persevere we can be understood.

Blessed are you who walk with us in public places and ignore the stares of strangers, for in your companionship we find havens of relaxation.

Blessed are you who never bid us "hurry up" and more blessed who do not snatch our tasks from our hands to do them for us, for often we need time rather than help.

Blessed are you who stand beside us as we enter new and untried ventures, for our failures will be outweighed by the times when we surprise ourselves and you.

Blessed are you who ask for our help, for our greatest need is to be needed.

Blessed are you who help us with the graciousness of Christ, for often we need the help we cannot ask for.

Blessed are you when you assure us that the thing that makes us individuals is not our wounded nervous systems, not in our peculiar muscles, not in our difficulty in learning, but in the God-given self which no infirmity can confine.

Rejoice and be exceeding glad, and know that you give us reassurance that could never be spoken in words, for you deal with us as Christ deals with all his children.

Author Unknown

Contents

Heroes of a
Special Kind

The squeaking and squealing of sneakers against the wooden gym floor put my teeth on edge as I step into the crowded room. The floor hockey teams banter the puck back and forth fighting for control. "Come on, Jim. Push...just a little farther; you can do it. Keep going; you're almost there. Push, Jim, push!"

It's a sunny California morning and I'm attending my first Special Olympics floor hockey meet. I have no idea what to expect and am not prepared for the noise level. Loud cheers echo off the walls of the cavernous gym. Enthusiasm and joy fill the building.

Earlier this morning I received a call to let me know that my son's team would be playing in Fallbrook, a neighboring town. Joel lives in a private home for the developmentally disabled in Lakeside, California, an hour from our home in Vista. Most of the time his

Special Olympics events are far from us, so this is my first opportunity to see him in action.

Joel has cerebral palsy and walks with some difficulty, but I am told he is doing well as a floor hockey player. Today I am excited to finally see how he maneuvers around a hockey floor.

As I try to adjust to the noise, I peer around the gym looking for Joel. There must be 20 teams waiting their turn at play.

I spot his group situated on the stage level of the multipurpose gym and ease myself into the crowd, hoping Joel won't see me so I can observe his interaction with the guys. No such luck. He darts toward me in his stumbling run, excitedly hollering, "Mom, Mom....Hi, Mom!" How I love the sound of those familiar faltering words.

We sit side by side, feet dangling over the side of the stage, watching the action. Those playing are in the higher-functioning division, several with Down syndrome, and they're good! With both teams equally matched, the opponents strain and fight for control of the puck. Sweat pours down their faces, and they grunt like the pros. A goal is made and both sides cheer, the competitiveness replaced with honest joy in each player's success. The "high five" is given all around.

Under massive helmets, wide grins spread from ear to ear. Some of the players jump up and down excitedly. Every time a goal is made, scoring players get pats and hugs from both teams before play resumes. Finally the buzzer sounds, and the players strut off the floor with a sense of importance, again enveloped in hugs, this time from their coaches. Helmets are pulled off sweaty heads; arms are raised in victory. The cheering is deafening.

Now it's time for my son's team. I watch with a thrill as my lanky 26-year-old puts on his helmet and grabs his stick. "See me, Mom!" *Yes, my darling son, I see you with my heart full of love.*

Now I observe the real heroes of this day. Special Olympics coaches are out in force for these younger athletes in the lower-functioning division, giving last minute instructions. "Joe, you run this way with the puck." "Sam, you can't sit down in the middle of the playing floor; get up! Put your stick on the floor; don't swing it around in the air." "Okay, everyone have fun!"

The buzzer sounds, but nobody moves! The players stand idle, sticks in hand, puck on the floor. Coaches begin to holler, "Okay, you guys, get the puck, get the puck." "Joe, take your stick and hit it; MOVE!"

Bobby ambles toward the puck and manges to put his stick on it. The coach yells, "Push it, Bobby! Come on, Bobby, you can do it; PUSH! That's the way, keep going; push, Bobby, push!"

Bobby looks at his coach, transfers his stick to his weak hand, grins, and waves the free hand. Transferring the stick again, he looks at the puck. With deep concentration he places the stick on top of the puck and moves it a few inches and then a few more, while the coach, hunkered down at the sidelines and dripping with sweat, cajoles and encourages, willing Bobby to move.

A player from the other team meanders to the puck, gently shoves Bobby's stick away with his own, takes over the puck, and inches it in the same direction. His coach yells, "You got it, Scottie! Go the other way, Scottie; turn around. Push it the other way. Our goal's on the other end!" And so the game goes until the buzzer sounds, ending the first half.

Exhausted from mentally trying to help the players move the puck, I observe the coaches. Wringing wet, they encourage their teams. "Great game, guys; you're doing good." "I'm so proud of you." They rub the player's backs as they talk and hug each one.

The buzzer sounds for the second half and off they go. Again the players stand and look at the puck, trying to get their brains to send the proper signals to their hands to move the stick one inch, then one more inch. Finally, Joel, in his stumbling gait, walks over to the puck and takes control with his stick.

I go crazy. "Come on, Joel, you can do it!" I

scream. "Push hard; push, Joel, push!" He methodically inches his way along the court and is within range of the goal. The goalie is on the job, guarding the entrance. Joel begins to giggle, causing loss of concentration. He stops to think and again inches the puck along, making time stand still. The coaches jump up and down hollering, "Go for it, Joel; go for it!" as I wilt from the mental exhaustion of helping him move.

Just as the puck is inched into the net, the goalie moves into action. In what appears to be slow motion, he steals the puck. Joel turns to me with his impish grin, as if to say, "Oh, well, we all did good, huh, Mom!" and the buzzer sounds again. The game over, the players move off the court to their coaches, and players from both teams are welcomed as champions.

I drink in the excitement, my legs numb from dangling over the stage edge. The emotion is overwhelming. *Who are these volunteers who care so much for people who are handicapped? What makes them willing to spend their evenings and weekends lovingly instructing in such slow-paced learning situations?*

For years I have seen the coaches on news clips for Special Olympics. No longer are they nameless faces holding out their waiting arms at the finish lines; today I see "Special Heroes," who themselves deserve a hug.

Meet Our
Special
Heroes

Christine Miller Day

"These athletes, every day of their lives, get up and try again to meet the challenges of the day. And, do you know what? Every day they challenge me!"

Christine Miller Day

Christine Miller Day, since 1987, has been employed by Special Olympics for North San Diego County as assistant area director. Evenings and weekends she and her husband, Jim, can be found on the floor hockey courts with the many other volunteers and Special Olympians.

ORANGE DRINK RAN IN RIVULETS down her elbows and trickled into her pockets; she could feel the coolness as it ran down her legs. Chris Day stood in a pool of the sticky goo, and as she tried to move, her feet stuck to the floor.

Her job for the day was to dip a big pitcher into a vat of orange drink and pour it into waiting cups while Special Olympians filed by one by one. Sounds easy enough, but for these athletes this was one more feat to master.

Some of the hands that reached for the cups were twisted and only semi-useful. With great independence and deep concentration, the cups were carried away.

Occasionally, an athlete, jostled from behind or stumbling on the uneven ground, spilled orange drink on the table, on the ground, or on Chris. "I didn't know whether to help them or grit my teeth and allow the athlete to try to handle it alone," she mused. In any case, she had her hands full just trying to keep the table from tipping over.

As she dabbed at the mess in her hair, she asked herself, "Am I going to survive this lunchtime?"

A recent transplant to San Diego, Chris's idea of participating at this Special Olympics weekend was to meet new people, not stand around wearing orange drink.

Interrupting her thoughts, someone bellowed from across the field, "Chris!"

Chris jerked her head, and her eyes focused on a tall, lanky teenager from the T-ball game she had refereed the day before. He headed straight for her and quickly enveloped her in a bear hug, her first exposure to the affectionate nature of people with mental retardation. He was not the least put off by the orange drink that dripped from her body, and in his booming voice he said, "Hey, my friend, how are you today?"

"Suddenly, I was loving even the feel of the

sweet, sticky goo I wore, and I wanted to be involved in the future of Special Olympics and in the lives of these people."

Chris Day's blue eyes sparkled with emotion as she recounted her introduction to Special Olympics. A bundle of energy, she has difficulty these days getting up close to her desk. However, being eight and a half months pregnant with her first child has not dampened her enthusiasm for her job one bit. Her blond, curly head is always awhirl with the activities of the 20 different sports programs the North County office runs.

"I left the Greater San Diego Games that first weekend without realizing the experience had forever changed my life."

Chris was immediately recruited and trained as a volunteer assistant coach. For the next two years, she held that position, after which she became head floor hockey coach, a position she has held for the past eight years.

"I love it dearly," she says proudly. "When I began in 1980, we had one team; now we have five, plus two wheelchair teams!"

She and her athletes travel both winter and summer to state games. In 1987 they represented California in an international invitational floor hockey conference in Toronto, Canada. Twenty-two teams competed: one

"At that moment I experienced
one of the most exhilarating times
of my life. I realized then that the
time I had spent with Jeff had
really counted!"

from Denmark, ten from the U.S., and eleven from Canada. Chris's team took fourth place.

Working both as a paid staff member and as a dedicated volunteer, Chris definitely has her hands full. Keeping coaches informed and athletes motivated is only a part of her job. She also speaks at local service clubs and churches, enlisting more and more volunteers for the ever-growing Special Olympics program. Then, at the end of her work day, on Tuesday evenings and weekends, she can be found in her volunteer capacity as floor hockey coach at the National Guard Armory, always encouraging, teaching, prompting, and hugging her very special friends.

Speaking with deep emotion she continued, "Special Olympics is about people, retarded people. Their successes are some of the sweetest anywhere.

"Take Jeff, for instance. Jeff and his brother Chris both have mental retardation. Chris, the higher-functioning of the two, was assigned to a more advanced team. Jeff is very, very slow. His minimal speech consists of a hesitant yes or no." Chris has learned to ask questions that can be answered with one or the other because it's the only way to get a response. Jeff's low comprehension allows him to respond to only one command at a time, so training is slow and tedious. One thing he can do is smile, a wide, warm, loving grin that lights up his face and makes you want to grab him and hug him tight.

Chris spent the seasons of 1983 and 1984 with Jeff under her wing. Standing behind him with her hands on his hips, speaking into his ear, she coached, "Okay, Jeff, let's move the stick to the right, okay?"

"Yes," he would say with a grin.

"Now, let's move to the left. Watch, now, here comes the puck." Every practice, week after week, she stood behind him repeating those same words.

"For the entire season I took him out on the court and placed him in his position. He never moved from that spot! He might or might not touch the puck, but he never, ever moved a foot."

At the start of the second season, occasionally Jeff would move, largely by accident. Needless to say, the majority of the shots whizzed past him.

Chris smiled and wistfully recalled an unforgettable experience. "In January the team was at the San Diego Invitational Tournament. It was the last game of the second day. The winner of this game would receive the gold medal.

"My team was hyped. We had won two games and felt sure we could go 3 and 0. When the game ended, we were tied and went into overtime. This consisted of two three-minute lines.

"At the end of the two lines, the teams were still tied. The next step was sudden death and the first team to score would be the winner.

"Everyone was excited. Energy was so high, the air seemed electrified! I was beside myself, wringing my hands, pacing the floor. The coach on the other team was in worse shape, running up and down the sidelines. Parents were standing in the bleachers, waving their arms and hollering. The athletes, as always, were taking the whole scene in stride and looking at the coaches and spectators as if we were very strange.

"The whistle blew for the sudden death. Immediately the opposing team got the puck and whizzed it toward the goal. Their best player captured the puck and made a shot, shoving it as hard as he could toward the goal. Suddenly from nowhere, one of my players blocked the puck and sent it shimmering down the floor straight for Jeff.

"My heart stopped, and I thought, 'Oh, no, we've lost for sure!'

"Jeff looked up and a magnificent grin lit up his face. He waited until the puck swooped in front of him. Then, placing his stick right in the center of the puck, he lunged down the court and slammed it into the goal.

"All movement came to an abrupt halt. The audience stood, stunned.

"Silence fell. For a long second everyone tried to comprehend what had just happened. Then the crowd, the teams, and the coaches exploded into one giant, wild cheer.

"Jeff lifted his head and turned to me with a knowing smile. If I could have heard his words, I feel sure they would have been, 'See, Chris, I knew I could do it; I was just waiting for the right time.'"

Chris breathlessly continued, "At that moment I experienced one of the most exhilarating times of my life. I realized then that the time I had spent with Jeff had really counted!"

She readily confesses she is addicted to the love and energy she receives from the athletes. "It's a real high. I don't know what I would do without them in my life. My involvement is very rewarding, fulfilling, and personal."

Chris says she realizes that she is giving back to the community and is, hopefully, making a difference in other people's lives, but that has become secondary to the energy and life-force she receives from being part of Special Olympics.

A catalyst in involving other members of her family in Special Olympics, as well, she enlisted her dad, Chris Miller, as her head gofer. She exclaimed, "I'd be lost without him! He's in my office every day, fixing broken things, moving desks, hanging pictures, sweeping floors, organizing supply closets, etc. And he loves to interact with the athletes."

The love she has for her dad radiated as she continued, "He is at our state games every year helping to do the time-consuming, but necessary, things like taking kids to the bathroom, wiping their noses, washing their hands and faces, corralling wanderers, getting uniforms on and off, packing and unpacking bags—simple but vital things that must be done for those who cannot do for themselves. He goes home exhausted, but without complaints."

When Chris married her husband, Jim, he was in no way involved with Special Olympics. Now he also is totally committed, currently serving as Special Olympics head referee for the state of California and as one of Chris's floor hockey coaches.

Thoughtfully, Chris reflected, "My core belief is that you get out of life what you put into it. Therefore, I want to give it my all. People with mental retardation are here to help us learn. They are excellent teachers. They are so 'in the moment,' so full of love and trust. They have no prejudice; they have no inhibitions; they are willing to try *one more time,* so much more than those termed 'normal.' "

She asks, "How many people would get up everyday for five or six weeks to learn or relearn how to tie their shoes? A 'normal' person would try for two or three days and, not succeeding, would buy Velcro or slip-on shoes. These athletes, every day of their lives, get up and try again to meet the challenges of the day. And, do you know what? Every day they challenge me!"

If I Can

If I can stop one heart from breaking,
I shall not live in vain;
If I can ease one life the aching,
Or cool one pain,
Or help one fainting robin
Unto his nest again,
I shall not live in vain.

—Emily Dickinson

Darryl Chunestudy

"My kids are great to work with. We have fun together. I try to teach them we are a team with no 'hot dogs'; we are all in the sport together."

Darryl Chunestudy

Darryl Chunestudy, "Chooch" to the people of Jay, Oklahoma, was the 1988 Oklahoma Special Olympics Coach of the Year. Presently he coaches all Special Olympics sports for the Jay, Oklahoma, special education program.

"DARRYL WAS ON HIS WAY to reform school just a few short years ago," relates his substitute mother, Jan Davis. "In fact, that first week of working with him at school, I wouldn't have given him a snowball's chance!"

The director of the Jay, Oklahoma, special education program, Jan can't remember the day Darryl moved into her home, but she can recall vividly how he has moved into her heart. Jan lovingly recounts how much Darryl has come to mean to her and to the people of this little town in northwest Oklahoma.

When Darryl happened on the scene at Jay High School, he was a belligerent, angry young boy with boundless energy, which teachers knew would have to be channeled quickly or they would all be in trouble. Study habits were nonexistent and the chip on Darryl's shoulder was more like a beam. He had the body of a full-grown man, and his Cherokee blood had a low boiling point.

One of eight children, Darryl grew up in rural Oklahoma, in the foothills of the Ozarks, amid lush, green vegetation and hot, humid summers where the red clay bakes into the ground like pottery. His mother worked at a local nursing home to keep food on the table for her family, and the sheer logistics of caring for a family of eight children didn't leave much time for social interaction. Outside of basic necessities, the siblings were on their own as to the molding of much of their character—hence, in this case, the angry young man who presented himself one day to Jay High School.

It became apparent immediately that Darryl was a natural athlete. Because of his lack of social skills, he was channeled into the Special Olympics teams, and for the years until he was 21 he continued to play baseball, softball, and basketball on those teams.

His interaction with the slower, lower-functioning boys on the teams began a mellowing process within Darryl, and before long he became their champion. More and more he was called on by coaches and teachers to intercede on behalf of a teammate or a classmate, and before long he became "Chooch," local hero.

Darryl's graduation from high school was a milestone, due largely to countless hours of loving tutoring and nurturing by teachers at Jay High School. The first high school graduate in his entire family, he was quickly recruited by those same teachers as a Special Olympics coach. Before long he became *the* Special Olympics coach.

Virginia Hare, work-study teacher, says, "Energy, capability, and understanding are only three of the attributes I associate with this young man whose own athletic ability has been instrumental in his upward climb to maturity, emotional stability, and personal growth. Darryl is a product and graduate of the work-study program that I coordinate at Jay High School. We, his teachers, recognized much potential in this young boy, who on the road to fruition, would need an extra amount of guidance, counsel, patience, and time.

"Today we see the results of our work. Watching Darryl work and train with our Special Olympians brings joy to my heart, for in his actions of love and understanding, he helps to establish confidence and determination and a sense of harmony in these young lives."

Jan Davis said, "Laughter is a constant companion when Darryl works with students. He has taught by example that all people are human and subject to error, but that self-castigation is useless. This young

"Watching Darryl work and train
with our Special Olympians brings
joy to my heart, for in his actions
of love and understanding, he
helps to establish confidence and
determination and a sense of
harmony in these young lives."
                              —Virginia Hare

man has learned one of life's lessons that many of us never learn—that failing at something is not a defeat, but instead can be a catalyst toward renewed effort. Our students look up to Darryl as their coach, their friend, their protector, and their hero!

"In my heart, this young Cherokee Indian is Special Olympics Coach of the Century!"

Jay, Oklahoma, is so proud of their Special Olympics athletes that they had a contingent of parents and fans accompany them to the International Games in South Bend, Indiana.

Some of the kids had never been out of Oklahoma, or Jay, for that matter. This look at the larger world was a fascinating experience for them. In giving directions for meeting at a certain spot one day, one of the athletes said to a teacher, "Meet me where the waterfall shoots straight up in the air!" He had never seen a fountain before.

One of Darryl's Special Olympics athletes, Audie Woolman, writes of him, "If we are ever getting beat he stays calm and cool. He doesn't get mad. He helps us individually, and if you need help he will stay after practice or any other time and help you practice to get better. No matter what happens in a game, whether we lose or win, he wants us to show sportsmanship afterwards. If we need a ride home after practice, he takes us; it doesn't matter how far it is. Darryl gets along with everybody. He has fun at whatever he does. He works real good with kids, and we enjoy him coaching us and being our friend."

As Darryl continues his work with Special Olympics, he also continues to improve as an athlete. He has survived three cuts with the Cincinnati Reds ball club and is awaiting word on a Houston trip to play in a try-out tournament for their Double A team.

A young man of few words, Darryl quips, "My kids are great to work with. We have fun together. I try to teach them we are a team with no 'hot dogs'; we are all in the sport together. We got so good at working together that Oklahoma Special Olympics had to make a new division for us and a few other teams on our level."

Minutes of Gold

Two or three minutes—two or three hours,
What do they mean in this life of ours?
Not very much if but counted as time,
But minutes of Gold and hours sublime,
If only we'll use them once in a while
To make someone happy—make someone smile.
A minute may dry a little lad's tears,
An hour sweep aside trouble of years.
Minutes of my time may bring to an end
Hopelessness somewhere, and bring me a friend.

—Author Unknown

Paul Samuel Epstein

"I gain more from my association with Special Olympics athletes than my athletes will ever gain from me. I get to work with real winners who have true spirit…"

Paul Samuel Epstein

Paul Samuel Epstein is a sergeant with the Metropolitan Police Department in Honolulu, Hawaii. In 1990 he was chosen one of the ten best volunteers in Hawaii and was honored with the prestigious Thomas Jefferson Award. Paul directs the annual Troy Barboza Law Enforcement Torch Run, bringing together more than 1,000 law enforcement officials each year for this fund-raiser.

THE WARM HAWAIIAN SUNSHINE BATHES Paul's suntanned face as he reflects on his work with Hawaii Special Olympics. Waikiki is surprisingly quiet on this November afternoon as he walks slowly down the beach alone gathering the thoughts he plans to share on this important part of his life.

"My first exposure to Special Olympics came in 1981, as a result of a class project for our Honolulu Police Academy. We were required to donate time to some kind of community service organization, and our group chose to work at the Hawaii Special Olympics State Games.

"Originally we were supposed to do security and crowd control. But as soon as I arrived, I knew I didn't want to be involved with security; I wanted to be a hugger and work with the athletes. Since that very first day in 1981, I have been actively involved as a coach, a hugger, and a supporter of Hawaii Special Olympics."

As a basketball and soccer coach, Paul has had opportunities to travel with his athletes to many places. His soccer team of 13 went to the International Games at the University of Notre Dame in South Bend, Indiana, during the summer of 1987. In March of that same year, they went to the Island of Kauai to play the Kauai High School basketball team.

Paul has traveled to San Francisco and to Florida carrying the torch for Special Olympics. He has also been the Torch Run director for the state of Hawaii for three years. In 1988, this involved over 600 runners, all law enforcement officers, running for Special Olympics. A three-day run, this precedes the lighting of the torch for the summer games.

Paul's soccer team, the Rainbows, is comprised of 22 athletes who have mental retardation. They are the 1988, 1989, and 1990 state of Hawaii champions, a gold medal team.

"The young athletes I coach are the pride of my life," says Paul. "At the 1987 International Games, our team was in the last heat. They had played five hard games and were in the final stretch for the medal. Lamar Tuiono was our fullback (the player directly in front of the goal). Lamar, a defensive player, has cerebral palsy (CP) in addition to his other health problems. The CP causes him to have very poor balance, especially on one side, as one leg is a bit shorter than the other.

"Lamar is a super kid with real spirit. In all the games we play, if a striker or a forward for the other team bumps against Lamar, we can almost be sure he will hit the floor with a thud. However, he hurriedly picks himself up and gets back into the game.

"In this particular game, tension on the field was thick as we were down to the wire for the medal. Lamar concentrated hard on staying on his feet and holding the fence as he guarded the goal. The spectators were screaming and the coaches were sweating profusely as the electrically charged tension became almost unbearable.

"Charging down the field, the Connecticut team's striker barreled down on Lamar and plowed right into him. For once, it was the other team player who hit the floor and not Lamar. Surprised, he looked over at me. I knew this gave our team the advantage. Lamar looked down at the poor guy who was spread

"...losing by 20 points didn't matter at all. What mattered was the people watching them, the fans who were cheering them on, and the team working hard for any accomplishment..."

out on the floor and without hesitating a second, he stooped down and with his one good hand helped the player up. That player, once on his feet, was more agile than Lamar and immediately had the advantage.

"This tender act of compassion on the part of our Hawaii player made me, the people in the stands, and all our athletes reflect that it was not our getting the ball and the advantage that was paramount. From Lamar's point of view, a human being had fallen down and he had to help him up. The game suddenly took on a whole new meaning for each player, and fan as well, for we had all been joined in a beautiful experience."

Paul recounts another experience at the Hawaii state basketball finals at King Kamehameha High School. "Equipped with only seven team members, the players were playing their hearts out, their faces red from exertion and hair drenched with perspiration. But play as hard as they might, they were still 20 points behind. I have never seen a bunch of guys play harder. Back and forth they ran up and down the court, never giving up. Finally, the buzzer sounded and the game was over.

"One of the athletes, Tyler Dumas, sopping wet and grinning from ear to ear, ran over to me and said excitedly, 'Great game, great game, coach; who won?'

"That was it. Imagine that! To Tyler and the other

athletes, losing by 20 points didn't matter at all. What mattered was the people watching them, the fans who were cheering them on, and the team working hard for any accomplishment—to get that inbound pass, to make those rebounds. The score didn't matter. Getting out there and accomplishing what they could is what mattered. Almost as an afterthought to a great game, the question 'who won?' had little significance."

A very important aspect Paul has discovered is that Special Olympics can help kids who are disadvantaged— not necessarily people who are mentally retarded, but rather people of average to high intelligence. As a police officer, he works with many kids who lack self-esteem and self-confidence and who are into drugs and crime. When Paul talks to these juveniles, they really don't know anything about giving or helping to build something. They only know how to take from society.

Paul has brought some of these kids to Special Olympics practices with him. He tells them, "Here are people who are mentally disadvantaged. Help them."

"Invariably, on those occasions when I bring juvenile offenders to my practices, they come back to me and say they love helping other people. They're on their best behavior and really shine through. It's a spiritual thing to watch.

"Real criminals—juvenile criminals—come to Special Olympics practices to try to help our athletes, and when they do, these juveniles begin to feel good about themselves. Once that happens, they are dealing from a source of strength, not weakness. With this strength they can go out and learn to become good, productive citizens."

Paul's past eight years of involvement and coaching a team of 22 athletes have been a source of unending satisfaction to him. "I'm finding out that through athletics people with mental retardation build self-esteem and self-respect and feel a sense of accomplishment. This is so readily visible from the athletes on my team."

One mother came to the coaches and said, "My son was never able to ride a bus by himself. I never thought he would be able to do that. But now he is." Sure enough, the athlete is not only on the bus, the athlete is going to work.

One day a mother telephoned and exclaimed, "Cory has graduated from McDonald's cooking school. He is going to be a full-time cook at their restaurant. I can't believe he is actually going to be a cook!"

At the next practice, as is the custom, athletes and coaches joined hands in a circle and greeted each other and any new people in the group. They also talked about the past week's accomplishments. Paul announced, "Cory graduated from cooking school!" Everyone clapped and grinned with great pride for one of their own. "The incredible absence of jealousy with these athletes always warms me," muses Paul.

Teachers call frequently to let Paul know how much better their students are doing in their classroom work as a result of Special Olympics involvement.

It has been Paul's experience that Special Olympics coaches interact with their athletes; they never talk down to them. Practices are scheduled to instruct and work with athletes, to allow them to be a part of the structure.

Paul reflects, "I gain more from my association with Special Olympics athletes than my athletes will ever gain from me. I get to work with real winners who have true spirit, who do things because they want to do things. To witness the joy and honesty of the lives of these athletes is a gift I receive. They help me to understand life. I simply show my appreciation for their help by working with them. It is truly a reciprocal relationship."

For Whom the Bell Tolls

*No man is an island entire of itself.
Every man is a piece of the continent, a
part of the main. If a clod be washed
away by the sea, Europe is the less, as
well as if a promontory were, as well as
if a manor of thy friends or of thine
own were. Any man's death diminishes
me, because I am involved in mankind.
Therefore never send to know for whom
the bell tolls. It tolls for thee.*

—John Donne

Erika Gans

"What lengths Special Olympics coaches will go to so their special people can experience life!"

Erika Gans

An adaptive physical education teacher at the Wester Elementary School in Livonia, Michigan, Erika (Rikki) Gans is the recipient of the 1988 Michigan Special Olympics Coach of the Year Award. That same year, she was named Special Olympics International Coach of the Year. Since 1974, she has served in a volunteer capacity as a local coordinator, member of the Area Management Team, and also coaches aquatics, poly hockey, gymnastics, soccer, track and field, team handball, and basketball. She and her husband, Marvin, are the parents of three grown children.

"I PICKED MY STEPS VERY CAREFULLY as I walked down the snow laden path," said Rikki. "Hearing a scooting sound behind me, I turned and laughed. There, sitting on the icy ground, was one of my best basketball players. He decided the safest way to get to our destination was to scoot."

The Michigan Regional Winter Special Olympics

made a great impact on Rikki's school that first time they competed with six of their highest-functioning athletes. Although Michigan is a winter state, most of Rikki's students had limited exposure to snow. At this event, her athletes had the time of their lives: tobogganing, ice block pushing, snow sculpting, tubing, sledding, snowshoe racing, and cross-country skiing.

"I couldn't believe my eyes when I observed one racing event," Rikki said. "Coaches had rigged up a set of skis with a wheelchair perched on top. A steering wheel was placed in front so the occupant of the wheelchair could steer. A coach stood on the skis behind the wheelchair as the entire contraption whizzed smoothly down the blinding white, snow-packed slope. Each taking his or her turn, the occupants of the wheelchair, bundled up in their brightly colored ski suits, toboggan caps, and mittens, looked completely enraptured as the icy wind blew against their red cheeks. Their joy spread to all who surrounded them as they slid to a halt at the bottom of the incline. I was afraid my face would freeze from the happy tears sliding down my cheeks as this scene unfolded. I thought I had seen it all before, but I believe this event will never be surpassed. What lengths Special Olympics coaches will go to so their special people can experience life!"

Rikki's introduction to special education was quite left-handed. Upon returning to her school district after a leave of absence, she was told there were no openings for a gym teacher at either the elementary or high school level; however, there was one opening for an adaptive physical education teacher with the trainable mentally impaired. She had many reservations but needed a job and immediately discovered her niche.

"In 1973, my principal, Cliff Page, called me into his office and asked if I would take some of my students to a Special Olympics meet at Garden City. The concept of Special Olympics was new to me; however, I agreed to take a few of my higher-functioning students for the outing. Although this first meet was a far cry from the organized, well-run events of today, nevertheless, I was impressed, and before the day was out I had jumped in with both feet," she recalled.

Through the years, Rikki has experienced the thrill of victory and the agony of defeat. One such victory came with Robert Brown. "My athletes know they cannot go to an area meet in swimming until they can swim the length of a pool," she recounted. "However, after much pleading by Robert and his dad to allow him to enter the competition, I finally agreed to make an exception, and off we went. I was feeling pretty unsure about my judgment, but I watched the fears swirl away in the swimming pool as Robert started off with a determination I had never seen before. He splashed, kicked, and struggled—hand over hand,

"It is always nice to be appreciated. But I couldn't have done it without the support of the school staff, other volunteers and chaperones, the families of the athletes, and the enthusiasm of the athletes themselves."

stroke after stroke—and made it the entire length of the pool. He may not have been first in the competition, but he really taught me a first: Never underestimate the determination of your athlete and the extra adrenaline that flows at these competitive meets.

"Robert went on to become an outstanding swimmer and now swims all four competitive strokes very well. I have often wondered if his continued progress would have happened had I not allowed him to connect a readiness moment with the skill. *The thrill of victory. There is nothing like it!*"

For Rikki, one agony of defeat came at a state meet. "Mary Castner was one of my Down syndrome swimmers, going for the gold," Rikki shared. "She was entered in the breaststroke event. The starting gun split the air and the swimmers all dived into the pool. Excitement ran so high that, about a quarter of the way through the lap, most of the swimmers had broken into freestyle. Mary, much slower than the rest, continued in her well-executed breaststroke. All the other swimmers finished before her, but Mary was the only one who completed the race totally doing the breaststroke. At the awards presentation she was given a ribbon for last place. I, like a mother hen, marched up to the officials and said, 'What happened! She is the only one who completed the race with the proper stroke!' I was informed that the race went by time only.[1] Needless to say, I counted to fifty a couple of times. The only way I could get through it was to stop and realize that the judges were also volunteers and if it weren't for volunteers we would not have Special Olympics at all."

Over the past six years, Rikki and her staff have been successful in a mainstreaming project with a neighboring school, placing regular elementary students with those who are trainable mentally impaired in seriously thought out programs interspersed throughout the school year.

Rikki feels that mainstreaming is extremely important for the special education student and for the student who is not mentally impaired. Each can learn from the other. While most mainstreaming is well planned, some of the most noteworthy mainstreaming can happen incidentally, greatly benefiting all those involved.

Ann Munn is a good example. In 1979, she qualified for Special Olympics International in Brockport, New York. Ann could choose between a couple of sports and chose swimming. As Rikki had no pool for her to practice in that summer, she arranged for Ann to practice with an AAU (Amateur Athletic Union) swim team in the community. This was mainstreaming even before it was recognized as such. Everyone gained from the experience, in spite of dire predictions.

That summer, Ann learned to do her flip turn—

without doubt owing to some encouragement from the AAU swim team. When she went to Internationals, Rikki was not chosen to accompany Ann as her official coach. "I wouldn't have missed the event," Rikki said. "My husband and I arranged our vacation so that we could attend and camped next to Ann's parents. Luckily, I was able to work with Ann at the Brockport pool and help familiarize her with the surroundings, where she ultimately won a silver and a gold.

"It was also interesting watching the other nations. A Central American coach had a difficult time getting his team into the water. When I offered to help, he explained that his team was accustomed to swimming in the ocean and was leery of the pool."

Rikki's involvement with Special Olympics has been time-consuming and has only been possible due to the long hours of her husband, Marvin, who works in his own field of education.

The outstanding honor of first being named 1988 Coach of the Year for Michigan and then 1988 International Coach of the Year gave Rikki's family immense pride in her involvement. "I must admit I enjoyed my recognition," said Rikki. "It is always nice to be appreciated. But I couldn't have done it without the support of the school staff, other volunteers and chaperones, the families of the athletes, and the enthusiasm of the athletes themselves." Special Olympics is the dew on her rose.

Note:

1. Today it is not necessarily true that races go by time only. Rules are based on the International Sports Federation for each respective sport. Games Rules Committees are appointed for international, regional, chapter, and area games.

My Daily Prayer

If I can do some good today,
If I can serve along life's way,
If I can something helpful say,
Lord, show me how.

If I can right a human wrong,
If I can help to make one strong,
If I can cheer with smile or song,
Lord, show me how.

If I can aid one in distress,
If I can make a burden less,
If I can spread more happiness,
Lord, show me how.

—Grenville Kleiser

Michael Paul Roderick

"I have a...justifiable admiration for the individual athlete or any person, for that matter, who adopts a personal challenge to be the best that he or she can be."

Michael Paul Roderick

Michael Roderick is a professor and technical director of theater at Bowdoin College in Brunswick, Maine.

"GEORGE O'KEEFFE SAYS IT MUCH BETTER than I," stated Mike. " 'Where I was born and where and how I have lived is unimportant. It is what I have done with where I have been that should be of interest.' I am puzzled how any person could possibly consider a contrary person such as myself as a 'Special Hero.' "

In the fall of 1967, Michael Roderick was a freshman in college. Several afternoons a week he spent time in a special education class, teaching art, crafts, French, and home skills like cooking and cleaning. The teacher in charge, Mickey Boutillier, subsequently became the founder and president of the Maine Special Olympics program. "I was there when it happened and trust that as long as there is some use for me, I will continue to be there in the future," Mike said.

The summer of 1968, at Mickey's request, Mike

worked at Camp Waban, a summer day camp for children and adults with mental retardation. Founded by Wayne Wormwood and friends, who believed in the equal rights of persons with mental retardation, the camp offered the full range of summer sports that you might expect at other camps, such as sailing, music, performing arts, and physical education.

In July of that year, *Sports Illustrated* magazine featured an article inviting special educators, coaches, and athletes to bring their athletes who were mentally retarded to Soldier Field in Chicago for the first Special Olympics Summer Games. Mickey took along several campers from Camp Waban. While the Games were far from perfect, the whole notion was a good one. Mickey returned enthusiastic about the possibilities. That enthusiasm enveloped Mike as well.

"That is a long way 'round Robin's barn to answer the question of my involvement with Special Olympics," said Mike. "Basically, it grew out of my friendship and association with Mickey Boutillier. Someone had to be able to type; I can, but with only two fingers. Someone had to have time off to help stuff and seal envelopes; I did. Someone had to be willing to act on his conviction; I was, and trust I still am.

"I am not an athlete, never have been, and expect that I never shall be. I have age on my side to guarantee the latter. I have a compulsive but justifiable admiration for the individual athlete or any person, for that matter, who adopts a personal challenge to be the best that he or she can be."

Mike learned, among other things, that persons who are not able to advocate for themselves require someone to advocate for them. He is one of hundreds of thousands of such advocates.[1]

"Not the best, nor the most qualified," admitted Mike, "I am involved with Special Olympics because it is selfishly fulfilling. Not because it is the fashionable thing to do, but rather because it is the right thing to do and it brings me great pleasure. I will continue my work as long as there is a need for someone to stuff and seal envelopes, run a duplicating machine, work fund-raising concessions, make signs, lug sports equipment, decorate banquet halls, wash dirty laundry, clean rooms, load buses, do typing, do artwork, lug tables, lug more chairs...and cheer on an athlete."

Mike is that special breed of volunteer who is not a Special Olympics coach; rather he is a gofer.

"I go fer this and I go fer that," said Mike. "During the last few years, I have had, unfortunately, less contact with the athletes. My work is, as it should be, well behind the scenes. It is where I am most comfortable and useful."

From the 20 years Michael Roderick has been affili-

"There is associated with all my involvement in Special Olympics a condition which causes my spirit to soar at the smallest accomplishment by any athlete. Personal accomplishments are not taken lightly in Special Olympics."

ated with Special Olympics, several stories came to mind. One story was from the 1983 International Special Olympics Summer Games in Baton Rouge, Louisiana.

"My responsibilities included caring for several athletes," Mike said. "I brought them to the staging area of their competition venue. One athlete, Rob—who also has cerebral palsy (CP)—stood a monolithic six feet, three inches. Rob was entered in the 200-meter run. He was not, as you might imagine, in the higher ability grouping of this event. However, he did have several things going for him most of the time.

"First, Rob had a sense of humor. He had learned to use humor as a disarming device to those who would, for example, be awkward when attempting to shake his hand.

"Second, he had patience. Rob preferred to spend more time in doing for himself what would have taken less time for others to do for him, such as putting on a pair of socks.

"His on-track event was scheduled for mid-afternoon. Rob's group, who were to run the 200-meter heat, marched onto the field to the starting line. He looked forward to this particular event most especially, because it was one of his best.

"The athletes assumed the starting position. The starting gun fired. With perspiration running down his face from the humidity of a Louisiana summer day, Rob moved hard toward second place. He strained forward with everything he had as he neared the 100-meter mark.

"Suddenly, tripping over his own foot, he tumbled head over heels on the very hard, all-weather track. In a flash, it was over. Track officials and medical personnel ran to his side to make sure he was not injured in the fall.

"Slowly and carefully, the officials returned Rob to the venue staging area following his heat's award ceremony. As he limped by, he turned to me and said, 'Well, that's the way the CP tumbles!' He grinned his crooked grin and wistfully looked back at the track, oblivious to the bandage on his left knee.

"Rob's Maine delegation was housed on the same floor as that of the Belgian group during the games. That afternoon, after conferring with all coaches and athletes, the head of the Belgian group called a floor meeting, requesting all residents to attend. With much pomp and circumstance, the delegation called Rob forward. Their spokesperson, in a booming voice, said, 'Rob, you fell, but in recognition of the courage you demonstrated on the athletic field a few hours ago, we have a special award for you.' With appropriate ceremony, one of their athletes stepped smartly forward and solemnly placed a Belgian Special Olympics Medal around Rob's neck. A cheer went up around the room for this courageous and witty young man."

Mike continued, "There is associated with all my involvement in Special Olympics a condition which causes my spirit to soar at the smallest accomplishment by any athlete. Personal accomplishments are not taken lightly in Special Olympics.

"My sense of wonderment grows in proportion to the small forward strides made by these special people. They are proof that as long as someone believes in you, it is always possible to achieve. Without that sympathetic conviction, the individual will struggle more for less. With it, he will struggle more for more and continue the struggle."

Note:

1. Special Olympics has subsequently addressed the issue of advocacy in their Athletes for Outreach program. See the Special Olympics section in the back of this book for additional information.

Rebecca McKee

"Special Olympics is the only place I know where a person is rewarded for his or her best effort."

Rebecca McKee

Rebecca McKee is an adapted physical education teacher in Lees Summit, Missouri. Her workday includes a one-hour adapted P.E. class at both the high school and junior high, with the remainder of her day spent teaching regular P.E. classes at an elementary school. Named Missouri Outstanding Special Olympics Coach for 1988, Rebecca also received "The People Who Make A Difference" Award given by USA Today and was featured in the December 1988 issue of that publication.

"WHEN I RECEIVED TWO TICKETS to a Special Olympics fall banquet, I had no idea what to expect," said Rebecca. "I was in my second year of teaching and was involved with my first adapted P.E. class. Adapted physical education involves students who cannot participate in a regular class because of severe motor limitations, mental handicaps, physical problems, or obesity. One of my students accompanied me to the dinner. There I sat, my senses soaking up all the speaker conveyed."

At that dinner, keynote speaker Jack Rudnay, former center for the Kansas City Chiefs football team, was having difficulty speaking because of the huge lump that almost filled his windpipe. As unchecked tears coursed down his cheeks, he said, "Of all the athletic competitions I have been involved with, Special Olympics is the purest."

This event marked the culmination of a year's hard work on the part of Special Olympics athletes. It was their night to shine before family and friends. As their names were called, some of them stumbled to the platform with palsied gait; some struggled along on braces and metal crutches; a few wheeled themselves with an agility that only comes with years of practice; some, with no physical limitations, bounded up on the platform. All had unbridled joy radiating from their faces.

After the benediction was given by one of the athletes, Rebecca also had a huge lump lodged in her throat. At that moment, she promised herself that all the athletes in her Special Olympics program would be in attendance at the next banquet.

As the banquet was fairly expensive, a yearlong appeal to local service clubs was launched to help with the expense involved. "Since that first banquet nine years ago, all my athletes who want to have been able to attend this event, thanks to the generosity of those service clubs," said Rebecca.

Rebecca became involved in Special Olympics as bus driver, member of the Kansas City Board, and area coordinator for the gymnastics event at the area Special Olympics Summer Games. She coaches bowling, basketball, gymnastics, track and field, pom-pom, and volleyball. She laughed and said, "My entire life revolves around Special Olympics."

Her family has found that if they want to be with her during a visit, they have to become involved also, often going on Special Olympics trips as chaperones. Her parents, brother, grandparents, and aunt have all been on trips. "My parents know my kids by name because I am always talking about them," said Rebecca.

"My brother is especially proud of my work with Special Olympics. He told me one time, 'When I get down and out, I think of some of the kids I have met through you—those who have had surgeries, those who struggle just to get through the day. It helps me get my head on straight.' "

Rebecca's eyes sparkled and her voice became husky with emotion as she shared some of the success stories of her athletes.

"The crowd stood and clapped as Dawn came by

"Tears streamed down the faces of most of the coaches as we reflected on the struggles our athletes had overcome to be at this place. There were no tears from the athletes. Incredible pride glowed from their faces as they waved to the people in the stands."

the grandstand. The other runners had long since crossed the finish line in the 200-meter dash event and were now a part of the crowd who were cheering noisily. Her face, wet with perspiration, split into a huge grin at the sounds from the stands.

"It was such a hot day, you could almost see the steam rising from the ground. Dawn's body trembled with exertion as she slowly—step by step—pulled her body along on her metal arm crutches. The effects of the cerebral palsy could be seen in the involuntary movements of her head. There, just ahead of her, was the finish line—and me. I was jumping, screaming, and crying from the sheer joy of watching this determined young woman finish her course. As she swung herself over the finish line, I swooped her up in my arms, almost toppling us both, and swung her around. 'Hey, world,' I said, 'here is a winner! Her name is Dawn Kella!' Immediately, we were surrounded by media people who also thought she was a winner."

"Kathy Trabue was chosen as Kansas City's Athlete of the Year in 1986 and was inducted into the Kansas City Athlete's Hall of Fame.

"The following year, she was selected to represent the state of Missouri in gymnastics at the International Games held in South Bend, Indiana. Graduation, moving away from home, securing a job, and practice for this upcoming event consumed this young woman who was mildly retarded. Sometimes I worried it would be too much for her; however, I could always count on her giving her all. I tried to give her as much slack as I could and still keep her on task.

"Finally, the big event arrived. To my great disappointment, I was not selected to accompany Kathy. So my faithful friend/volunteer and I paid our own way to South Bend to be on hand when Kathy arrived with the other athletes. Making the best of a bad situation, we wound up at a motel just across the state line (the closest accommodations we could find), and Kathy stayed in the dorm at Notre Dame.

"Our days were spent running her through her routines, rubbing her legs, walking her, talking to her, trying to inspire confidence within her spirit.

"The August day of the opening ceremonies was brilliantly clear and steamy hot. The stands were packed with spectators as the music began. Leading the parade around the field were two individuals carrying a gigantic archway of multicolored balloons. The athletes followed, prancing proudly, with the coaches bringing up the rear."

"What a spectacular moment!" Rebecca recalled. "Tears streamed down the faces of most of the coaches as we reflected on the struggles our athletes had overcome to be at this place. There were no tears from the athletes. Incredible pride glowed from their faces as they waved to the people in the stands.

"Kathy's events were floor exercise, balance beam, uneven parallel bars, and vaulting. The first day of competition was hard. She fell off the beam three times, and that was her best event. She was frustrated.

"Our biggest competitor was a cute little girl from Kansas. She and her coach and Kathy and I became good friends during the week, so we couldn't help rooting for her. When Kathy would get a gold in an event, this little girl would get a silver. And when Kathy got a silver, she got a gold. We were neck and neck.

"Going into the overall competition the last night, we felt Kathy had a pretty fair chance for a gold. During the day, she did an outstanding job on the balance beam, and her uneven routine was her best ever. We both regained some of the excitement that was lost the previous day. Our friend from Kansas also shined on her floor exercise. Once again, we were neck and neck. This was it!

"Nerves were taut. We paced, we jumped, we popped our knuckles—anything to relieve some of the tension. The vault was Kathy's last event. This would tell the story for the meet. The area was packed; many were cheering for Kathy. She had three trials to

"We like to win, but it isn't the most important thing. When we lose, we hop on the bus and ask, 'Where are we going to eat?'"

run and make her vault. The best of the three scores counted. Just this once I wanted it to be easy for her.

"The bell rang: first trial. Before I knew it, Kathy was off and running down the mat. Pow! She ran right into the horse. Miscalculating the distance, she hit the horse and flew over it, landing on her head. I held my breath for a minute. You could hear the crowd gasp. In a couple of seconds she was up and brushing herself off. My rigid body began to relax a little.

"The bell rang: second trial. This time she looked good as she ran down the mat. Oh, no! She caught her foot on the edge of the horse. Again, down on the mat. I heard her hit—hard. I ran and picked her up.

"Tears streamed down both our faces. I wanted so badly to tell her she didn't have to try again. 'Judge, please, can we have a minute?' I asked.

"The judge, emotion betraying his gruff manner, said, 'Yes, walk her around a minute; but she will have to make her third attempt.'

"We walked. 'Kathy,' I said, as I took her face in my hands, 'I love you. You know you are the only person who can make this vault. I can't do it for you. I would if I could. Maybe this would be a good time to talk to the Lord. You have depended on Him so many times in the past.' We took a minute while she did just that. When we went back to the runway, we were both calm and feeling more positive.

"The bell rang for the final trial. Off she ran, and this time up she sailed right over the horse with a flawless delivery. The crowd roared; I was wild! Even the judges got involved. It was complete bedlam as this young woman slowly lifted herself from the mat and blinked in disbelief.

"Wandering senselessly around the area with a fist full of numbers from each of her events, I tried to make my brain behave enough to calculate just where we stood. A coach from the state of Washington came to my rescue and grabbed the numbers from my hands. He calculated that Kathy had a good chance for a first in the overall competition—unless the Kansas girl edged us out by fractions.

"Wide World of Sports busily set up their equipment so they would be ready as winners were announced. The whole area was rigid with tension as we waited.

"At last the judge came to the microphone and said, 'Ladies and gentlemen, we have the results of the gymnastics overall competition.' The winner of the bronze medal was announced and proudly went forward to take her place on the award stand.

"Then, something odd happened. The judge continued, 'Ladies and gentlemen, there will be no second-place winner. Winner of the gold medal is not one, but two young ladies. We announce co-winners. Will the athlete from Missouri and the athlete from Kansas come forward and receive their gold medals!'

"The Kansas coach and I grabbed each other, danced around the gym, and rushed toward our dazed athletes. Moments later, as I stood watching these girls standing so composed and proud on the award platform, it was almost more than I could bear. I savored every moment of this once-in-a-lifetime thrill."

"Special Olympics also has its share of pom-pom girls," Rebecca shared. "Tracy Shelton was one. Confined to her wheelchair with cerebral palsy, the only way Tracy could experience the thrill of participating in Special Olympics was to wave her brightly colored pom-poms every time something exciting happened.

"Most of her life, Tracy had attended a state school for the mentally handicapped. She was in her freshman year of high school when she was moved to our public high school, and that's when I met her.

"In my work with her in Adapted P.E., I began to question whether, with the right surgery, Tracy might be able to walk. I had her standing on a treadmill rigged immovable. She could stand and walk a few steps. I consulted a physical therapist, and we put Tracy through a battery of tests. After looking over the results, he agreed with me.

"It was a battle to get this surgery. It was argued

that she wouldn't put out the effort to do all the exercises and lose the excess weight.

"Another teacher and I met officials of the center and Tracy's parents and really pushed. Our argument was 'Who are we to take the opportunity away from her if it's possible for her to walk!' Finally, in December 1986, she had the surgery.

"In April we had her on her feet. Graduation was fast approaching. However, we needed more time to work with her, so she agreed to allow us to hold her back one year. We set to work.

"She did a super job that next year, losing the needed weight and faithfully doing the exercises. It was a joy to see her hard at work fulfilling her goal. She walked, just a little, but she walked!

"Our pom-pom girl was graduating! She was determined to walk across the stage to receive her diploma. She asked if I would accompany her. I felt so honored.

"On graduation night, I picked her up at the center where she lived. She looked so pretty; her face flushed with excitement.

"To conserve her strength, we used her wheelchair to get her into the building. Some strong men picked her up—chair and all—and placed her on the platform.

"As I looked at the area, my heart sank. It was carpeted. Tracy had to scoot her feet as she walked. 'Will she be able to scoot on this carpeted floor?' I asked my-self.

"The auditorium was filled with parents and friends, each to see his or her special graduate. Finally, the superintendent began calling out the names. As he got closer to the S's, we stood her up and locked her braces in place.

" 'Tracy Shelton,' the superintendent announced. A chill started at the base of my spine and shot toward my head. Slowly—and laboriously—Tracy began try-ing to scoot her feet forward. They hardly moved an inch because of the carpet. After a few seconds, the drops of perspiration trickled down her cheeks, mak-ing tracks in her fresh make-up. 'It's okay, honey; let's just sit down. He'll bring it to you,' I whispered.

" 'No!' she said fiercely. She scooted her feet a few more inches. Finally, exhausted, she looked up at the superintendent, who by now was standing in front of her. Tears caused his face to sparkle under the bright lights. As he handed her the diploma, the audience rose as one person and gave Tracy a standing ovation. Look-ing out over her audience, she radiated her special courage to each person sitting there."

"I have a wonderful group of volunteers who are so supportive of me, the program, and our athletes," said Rebecca. "Donna Cheesman and Shirley Brummett are my right and left arms. Sometimes I feel like Moses; when I get tired, there they are, standing beside me ready to hold up my hands. Two wonderful men, Ron Hoduski and Ed Wilde, also help coach. We adults enjoy our comradery; in fact, sometimes we get downright silly.

"We like to win, but it isn't the most important thing. When we lose, we hop on the bus and ask, 'Where are we going to eat?' The kids are all so well-mannered—their social skills have improved greatly—that I would take them into the nicest restaurant any day and be proud of them.

"I have always felt it would be such a better world in which to live if we all were given credit for trying our best, if we were given a pat on the back for our efforts, even if we didn't win. Special Olympics is the only place I know where a person is rewarded for his or her best effort. The rest of the world doesn't reward effort. Too bad!"

Find your purpose and fling your life out into it; and the loftier your purpose is, the more sure you will be to make the world richer with every enrichment of yourself.

—Phillips Brooks

Flavol Glen Rester

"Being involved with Special Olympics keeps me involved with the human race, and I appreciate this special place of service."

Flavol Glen Rester

Flavol Glen Rester is program director at Millcreek Rehabilitation Center in Magee, Mississippi. He has served for the past five years as the area director for Area Two, Mississippi Special Olympics. Flavol and his wife, Kathy, have two sons, Reuben and Jared.

A CHURCH PIANIST WITH A DEGREE in music education, Flavol has never been inclined to sports but has always been inclined toward people. He laughs at his sports ineptitude. Rarely did he even attend a sports event—that is, until Special Olympics entered his life.

Flavol grew up in the home of a preacher, and the family traveled for many years as singing evangelists. He has maintained strong, loving ties with his family and God.

Flavol volunteered to be a chaperone for a Special Olympics event at the request of local teacher Dorothy Newsome. "I was enthralled by the festive atmosphere of the occasion," said Flavol. "The energy level and excitement of the event virtually electrified the air.

"There were approximately 400 athletes and some 200 sponsors, chaperones, and coaches at this event. This meet gave the athletes and me, brand new chaperone that I was, the time of our lives!

"In the fall of 1980, I became the Special Olympics coordinator for the entire Lawrence County—me, a non-athlete! Shortly after, I was certified as a gymnastics coach. I cooked, prepared athletes for international competition, served as ski coach, gymnastics coach, equestrian coach; anything that needed to be done, I did.

"I saw places I never would have otherwise: Colorado Springs, Myrtle Beach, Gatlinburg.

"In 1986 and 1987, I represented Mississippi at the 'Very Special Fishing' event sponsored by The Fishin' Hole with Jerry McKinnis at Lakeview, Arkansas, Gaston's White River Resort. I caught my first trout and had never even seen a rainbow trout before that. I took athletes with me who had never before fished in a river.

"In 1985, I saw the Smoky Mountains and took my first skiing trip. It seldom snows in southern Mississippi, and when it does there are no hills, so this was a unique experience for me. But even with all the things I have done and the places I have been, it is the athletes that hold me to Special Olympics.

"One of my earliest memories of actually making a difference in an athlete's life came when Sam appeared on the scene. He was an underachiever with little or no self-esteem. Constantly in trouble, Sam ran with a street gang, even though they were institutionalized. Every time you turned around they were into some petty crime, robbing candy or drink machines, stealing, or terrorizing the smaller children.

"Those who saw Sam flee the scenes of crimes noticed his great running ability, so we got involved with him and entered him in some running events. He started with the 200-meter race and always finished on top no matter whom he was running against. It was like he was being chased and wasn't about to be caught. We upped him to 400-meter races and the same thing happened. It was amazing. Finally, we put him in the mile run and he just kept going.

"The state office allowed the hiring of a paid sports director, who took a special interest in Sam and involved him in a state track club. Competing with non-handicapped people in his own age group, Sam rated in the top 10 in his division. It was phenomenal to see this young man run. He went from one kilometer to five. We tried to teach him to stay with the pack and not get ahead of them in order to pace himself. It was difficult, but he did learn the discipline and began bringing home trophies and plaques.

"The spiritual side of my life has grown immeasurably through Special Olympics. It's a privilege to work with parents and athletes who just need to be shown that someone really cares."

"In 1987, Sam was invited to participate in a mini-marathon sponsored by the United States Marine Corps in Washington, D.C. The coach, Becky Wells, who had worked with him in the institution went along. While the race was in progress, she stood at the side-lines awaiting the runners advancing toward her. She had talked with other coaches and, from figuring the times of the fastest individual athlete, expected to see him round the bend in about two minutes. But, to her astonishment, she looked up to see Sam rounding the bend, with no other runners in sight. Amid an up-roar from cheering and screaming fans, this young ath-lete won the race with over a two-minute lead.

"With his talent channeled, Sam, our delinquent, became a hero! What a thrill that was for all of us. When asked why he thought he won, Sam grinned and replied, 'When they said ready-set-go, I looked over at the fast guy and said to myself, I have to get in front of him. I took off and that's the last I saw of him!'

"Sam won all kinds of recognition for this feat. When he returned to Mississippi, he was on television and has been able to compete with the non-impaired all over the state and country. He has proven that in sports the developmentally disabled can compete.

"In 1983, as Lawrence County's coordinator, I had the option of picking two athletes to represent us at the summer games in Baton Rouge, Louisiana. I chose a young woman from the backwoods of our county. Mary Sue had never been out of the state of Mississippi. With no facilities available, we practiced tumbling in a field. Mary Sue never despaired when she fell or did a wrong move; she practiced and practiced and fell and practiced some more.

"She became a good gymnast and developed style, grace, and agility. She also developed a new sense of self-worth and confidence and soon her backwoods nickname 'Stink' was replaced with her given name.

"Having won gold medals at the State Games, Mary Sue was ready for the International Games in Baton Rouge. What an exciting trip for this young woman. Even the bus ride was an incredible adventure—full of new experiences. Upon our arrival at the campus of Louisiana State University, Mary Sue gaped at a group of young men, perhaps from the South Pacific, walking across campus with material draped around their waists like a skirt. Black Kenyans in native dress brought the same response.

"Mary Sue had stars in her eyes all week as she observed, felt, touched, and tasted life. But when her competition began in that enormous coliseum, with its bright lights, thousands of people, and blaring loudspeakers, she was so centered on her performance that it was as if the world had stopped and she were the only one in it. She won bronze medals and was completely thrilled, as were we.

"Whenever Special Olympics takes someone like Mary Sue and changes her into a bubbly person with a will to try things for herself, we are all winners."

"As a special education teacher, I had one student named Buck who didn't speak at all. For communication, he barked, a pattern learned from human isolation and primary interaction with the family dogs. As a result, Buck ran around the playground barking and biting the other children on the legs.

"We had a week-long Special Olympics skiing trip scheduled and, after much discussion, decided to allow Buck to accompany the group.

"I was not along on the trip so I can't say for sure what happened, but I was told that when Buck stepped off the bus he was a different kid. He could talk and was even a bit cocky. His confidence was above anything we had ever seen, as he laughed and talked with other classmates. He even began working toward his education. For weeks, Buck talked of what the trip had done for him, and even though I wasn't there, I felt very much a part of it. If one trip can make such a difference, imagine what is accomplished in the lives of nearly one million Special Olympians every year!"

Flavol reflected a minute before sharing his source of strength. "I was privileged to grow up in a family who believed in and taught of a personal relationship with Jesus Christ and am endeavoring to impart that to my own children. I know how Jesus loves children, and I feel privileged to help those with special needs. The spiritual side of my life has grown immeasurably through Special Olympics. It's a privilege to work with parents and athletes who just need to be shown that someone really cares.

"My family's awareness has been heightened as they see me helping people outside the church. I believe the church needs to be more active in serving and helping individuals with special needs."

Flavol paused briefly and then continued. "Sometimes it is difficult to prioritize my time and keep a proper balance in my relationship with God, my family, the church, and Special Olympics. Fortunately, I have a wonderful wife who is understanding and supportive. She feels as I do, that I am touching lives in a unique way. Being involved with Special Olympics keeps me involved with the human race, and I appreciate this special place of service."

I am only one, but I am one.
I can't do everything, but I can do something.
And what I can do, that I ought to do.
And what I ought to do, by the grace of God,
I shall do.

—Edward Everett Hale

Fredna Cross

"Spend one hour with these special-forever athletes and I guarantee they will win your heart—as they have mine."

Fredna Cross

Fredna Cross is the athletic director for Meridian Community College in Meridian, Mississippi. In 1988 she was the recipient of the Monsignor Burns Award. Married to her husband, Frank, for 36 years, they are the parents of two children: Frankie, now deceased, and Faye Ellen, graduate assistant in Special Education at the University of Southern Mississippi.

" 'B<small>RETT, PLEASE GO TO SLEEP</small>! You'll be too tired to run tomorrow if you don't get some rest.' Those words were so true, but I was also thinking of myself," shared Fredna. "I wasn't going to be worth a flip the next morning if I didn't get some sleep!"

Brett, Fredna's nonverbal athlete, was on his first trip away from home. For several hours she and her assistant director, Suzanne Timbrell, had coaxed Brett to go to sleep. "We brought him into our room to keep him from disturbing the rest of the athletes and were fast running out of ideas to comfort him. I tried singing, patting his back, and rubbing his head. Nothing worked! Finally, in desperation, we worked out a rotating shift so Suzanne and I could get a few hours of sleep!"

The sun shone brightly the next morning, and after breakfast and lots of black coffee the night was forgotten; there was too much excitement in the air. Later, Suzanne and Fredna had the immeasurable joy of standing with Brett as Governor William Winter of Mississippi slipped a gold medal around his neck. Seeing the joy on her young athlete's face made it worth every sleepless moment.

In 1967, Fredna worked as Director of Meridian Public School's Special Ed P.E., financed through a Kennedy Foundation Grant. During this time, she was invited to enter some of her TMR (Trainable Mentally Retarded) children in a track and field meet. In the Spring of 1968, 25 children attended the first State Special Olympics Meet. Fredna became enamored with this new, exciting opportunity and accepted the position of Area 5 District Director for Special Olympics.

"I had never been exposed to people with handicaps or mental retardation," said Fredna, "until our only son, Frankie, was born with hydrocephalus and was severely handicapped. He was bedridden throughout his 15 years of life. Through the love we shared,

I felt a need and desire to reach out to other handicapped youngsters. I learned so much of life from Frankie; it was my privilege to be his mother." Thus began a life's work for Fredna Cross.

Recently retiring from her volunteer job of 20 years as area director, Fredna continues with her teaching job and as a Special Olympics assistant director. For four years she directed a golf tournament fund-raiser that was extremely successful. Currently she is director of the area Athletics (track and field) meet and serves on the state board.

The athletes are Fredna's anchor to the organization. She recalls, "We were at a basketball tournament when one of my athletes, a small, quiet boy, complained that his feet hurt. He limped around the first day, moaning and whining, which was totally out of character for him. Finally, in desperation, I looked at his feet. They were red and hot to the touch. It occurred to me that we wore the same size shoes. I pulled off my 'tennies' and said, 'Okay Robbie, try these.' He put them on and breathed a sigh of relief. For the rest of the weekend, I limped around in his shoes. He was right, they hurt!"

"For the past five years," Fredna continued, "Mississippi's summer games have been held at Keisler Air Force Base where an airman or woman is assigned to each athlete as an escort. What a wonderful experience

"For so many years, people with retardation had to sit home and watch their brothers and sisters participate in sporting events. They wanted so desperately to be a part of life the way their siblings were but never had an opportunity until Special Olympics came along. Now these athletes have the opportunity to make their parents proud of them and their accomplishments."

for the athletes to have these important people in uniform walking around and eating with them. It has been an excellent encounter for the service personnel, as well.

Fredna is constantly amazed and gratified at the diverse personalities and the level of involvement of her volunteer staff. Eighteen of the teachers' aides in the elementary school P.E. program are active volunteers in Special Olympics.

Suzanne Turnbull, her former P.E. aide, went back to school and received a degree in special education. She now teaches a TMR class which is very active in Special Olympics.

Fredna also credits early involvement in Special Olympics as the motivating factor in her daughter's decision to become a TMR teacher.

She muses, "Sometimes I think Special Olympics is growing too fast. In the future I feel like the area directors are going to have to be paid career positions. It has definitely become a full-time job."

A woman of many interests, Fredna is an outdoor person who enjoys hunting with her pack of rabbit beagles. She also hunts deer and is an avid fisherwoman. In addition, she maintains a large garden at the country home she shares with her husband and their dogs.

"The 20 years I have spent working with Special

Olympics have provided joy that I cannot express in words. For so many years, people with retardation had to sit home and watch their brothers and sisters participate in sporting events. They wanted so desperately to be a part of life the way their siblings were but never had an opportunity until Special Olympics came along. Now these athletes have the opportunity to make their parents proud of them and their accomplishments.

"Although they have a limited capacity, the athletes are very grateful for all that is done for them and are quick to express their thanks to the volunteers for their help and love.

"The looks of joy and excitement expressed as they receive their ribbons and medals for their achievements are something that I will cherish forever.

"When I make speeches at service clubs, I challenge the audience, 'Spend one hour with these special-forever athletes and I guarantee they will win your heart—as they have mine.' "

Where your pleasure is, there is your treasure.
Where your treasure is, there is your heart.
Where your heart is, there is your happiness.

—Saint Augustine

The journey of a thousand miles begins with one step.

—Lao-tse

Barbara Ann Phillips

"Special Olympics has filled my inner needs. I haven't had time to think about growing old. There is always one more person I want to help reach their goal. In doing so, I have reached mine."

Barbara Ann Phillips

Barbara Ann Phillips is an instructional specialist in the Department of Special Education at the University of South Alabama in Mobile. Her husband has a mechanical contracting business. They are the parents of three grown children and grandparents of eight.

"MY HEART WAS IN MY THROAT as I stood at the edge of the track, watching her," said Barbara. "I felt such pride at the grace and style with which she ran.

"The breeze caught the fragile red ribbon that cordoned the finish line, causing it to shimmer in the sunlight. Streaking toward the ribbon, she was a front-runner by several yards when suddenly, unexplainably, she came to a stop. She stood within arm's length of the finish line and the red ribbon while another runner burst through causing the ribbon to flutter up and away from the mark."

Barbara ran to her and breathlessly asked, "Why didn't you run through the ribbon?"

She looked up, with perspiration running down her trusting young face, and said, "Daddy told me to be good and not break anything."

"I shall never forget that experience," Barbara recounted. "It taught me volumes about working with children and adults with mental retardation. Every detail must be explained with nothing taken for granted."

Barbara's work with trainable mentally retarded (TMR) children started even before the beginnings of Special Olympics.

"One summer day a friend telephoned to remind me I owed her a favor and she was ready to collect," said Barbara.

Her eyes sparkled as she remembered the favor that changed her life. "The next day found me at her pool surrounded by 30 TMR children eagerly waiting for me to teach them to swim. What an experience! As I looked from one to another, I felt overwhelmed, but we all jumped into the pool. At the end of that first session, I realized that this was a new beginning."

At the inception of Special Olympics in Alabama in 1968, Barbara Phillips was asked to participate and has been the aquatics director for the state, as well as area coordinator and coach, ever since. At the first meet, there were approximately 100 children; the officials were thrilled with the turnout, since public schools had few programs for handicapped children at that time.

"We took the children to Chicago for our first Special Olympics meet," Barbara said, "and I found there were many, many things I didn't know. I never dreamed we would have children who had never been on an airplane, never spent a night away from home, who didn't know how to adjust water in the bathtub or open sugar on the airplane. It was an exciting learning experience for both them and me! The joy of watching these young people grow and develop through these kinds of experiences has never diminished."

Barbara took one young man to the International Games held in Indiana, where they had a wonderful time and experienced the things of which she just spoke. Upon returning, she received a note from his mother that read, "I gave you a boy and you returned me a man."

That young man could swim his heart out, but more importantly, he also learned to bathe himself, shave himself, pick up his clothes, and many other daily living and socialization skills. "There is so much more to Special Olympics than competition," Barbara stated.

At the Alabama State Games, one of Barbara's swimmers was about to begin her heat when suddenly she sat down on the floor with her head in her lap. In

Barbara refers to her Special Olympics athletes as "my kids." It matters not if they are 40 years old or 10, they are still her kids.

a little voice muffled by the arms hiding her head, she cried, "I can't. I can't!"

Bending over her, Barbara said, "Be like the little engine that could; say I CAN. I CAN."

After winning, the athlete ran to Barbara and said, "I was like the engine that could; and I DID!"

In the early days of Special Olympics, it was often thought impossible for Down syndrome individuals to learn to swim. Never one to accept the word impossible, Barbara Phillips exhorts all those under her tutelage, "Don't say I can't; say, I'll try."

"One of my athletes was a Down syndrome boy who didn't know he couldn't learn to swim," said Barbara.

"He worked tirelessly, day after day. Some days he would pull himself out of the water, totally dejected at not being able to coordinate his arms and legs in the proper strokes; but he was always at the next practice, ready to try one more time. Finally, one day he pulled himself out of the water with a look of triumph on his face. He could swim!"

He became one of Barbara's strongest swimmers, winning medal after medal at local events. He grew and developed socially, and, finally, even represented Alabama at the International Special Olympics Summer Games.

Tragically, he died as a young adult. His mother

called Barbara soon after his death to tell her she was burying his Special Olympics medals with him, as they were the most precious things in the world to him. The mother shared proudly, "Those medals proved to my son that he did have worth and that he could do things that even many normal young people could not do. I'll always be grateful to you, Barbara."

Through the years Barbara has found that handicapped people far exceed nonhandicapped people in their quest to succeed. Her premise is that everyone doesn't have to win to be a success; they only have to try.

Due to Barbara's success with teaching young people with retardation to swim, she was asked to try water ballet with the goal of performing for the governor of the state of Alabama.

Over and over she repeated the simple commands to her team, "Raise your right hand, now your left hand; now turn around in the water." Day after day it seemed no progress was made, when suddenly it clicked.

"Jamie watched us work for a couple of weeks," Barbara said. "She wanted desperately to join us, but couldn't swim. Seeing the desire written on her face, I reluctantly said okay. It wasn't absolutely necessary that she be able to swim because the water was shallow. Jamie was jubilant and proved to be a very fast learner.

"Finally, the day arrived for us to perform in Montgomery for the governor. As I stood at the edge of the pool we were to perform in, my heart sank. It was too deep! There was no way Jamie could be a part of the program. When I brought her to the pool's edge to explain she couldn't participate, she looked up at me and defiantly said, 'I am, TOO!'

"She jumped into the water with the rest of the swimmers, and to my amazement for the next 30 minutes Jamie never missed a stroke."

Barbara has discovered through her years with Special Olympics that while you don't have to be a world-class expert in the sport you are teaching, you must have empathy for the athletes and the patience to take things in very small steps so they can follow.

Special Olympics inspired Barbara to begin a summer camp for people with handicaps. She served as camp director for eight years, teaching many things besides athletics—important things like social and housekeeping skills. At the same time, she gave parents a much needed respite.

Barbara refers to her Special Olympics athletes as "my kids." It matters not if they are 40 years old or 10, they are still her kids. She says with a laugh, "This is the grandmother in me."

Today, Barbara Phillips has no plans to retire from Special Olympics, but rather plans to train others to do some of the things she can no longer do. "Sometimes I think I scare people away," she said, "when they discover that in addition to my full-time job at the University, I put in a 40-hour volunteer week with Special Olympics. It certainly isn't a requirement; it's just me! Special Olympics has filled my inner needs. I haven't had time to think about growing old. There is always one more person I want to help reach their goal. In doing so, I have reached mine.

"My grandmother always told me, 'It isn't what you say that counts, it's what you do.' "

Do not pray for easy lives! Pray to be stronger men. Do not pray for tasks equal to your powers. Pray for powers equal to your tasks. Then the doing of your work shall be no miracle, but you shall be a miracle.

—Phillips Brooks

A task without vision is drudgery;
A vision without a task is a dream;
A task with a vision is victory.

—Author Unknown

Cristina Jean Henderson

"Special Olympics has gripped my life and I never plan to wrestle free."

Cristina Jean Henderson

A full-time student at San Diego State University, majoring in finance, Cristina has been involved as a volunteer coach with Special Olympics since 1988. Single, she lives outside San Diego, California.

"ROMANCE IS THE LAST THING I expected to find through Special Olympics," quipped Cristina Henderson. "I didn't have time for a boyfriend or a relationship—at least, that's what I thought, before I met Tim!"

Blond, curly hair framed her pretty face, and expressive green eyes revealed much about this vivacious young woman. Though normally on the move, Cristina comfortably settled her petite frame onto the couch in her sunny living room and reflected on her past year's involvement with Special Olympics.

Cristina met Tim Daly, a veteran Special Olympics coach, when she first began coaching. They chatted on one occasion and then didn't see each other again for three months. One evening they found themselves together on a bus filled with holiday cheer and excited athletes engrossed in the wonder of San Diego's Christmas lights.

"Tim told me he was attracted to me when he saw how intent I was on helping my athletes enjoy the evening," she recalled with a blush.

Cristina later discovered that it is a rather common occurrence for single people to meet through Special Olympics and fall in love. "It is easy to fall for someone you see is such a caring person, especially in this 'me first' world we live in today," she said.

Their relationship is growing every day as Tim and Cristina share their work with the athletes. Special Olympics is not a once-in-a-while volunteer effort, but a consuming, everyday commitment for both of these young people.

"When we are at tournaments," Cristina shared, "we are never together, because our athletes get top priority with each of us. However, we see one another in passing and holler encouraging words across the way; we are a built-in rooting section for each other."

Early on, Cristina found it nearly impossible to date someone outside Special Olympics, because most people don't understand her level of commitment. Being busy all the time and going to tournaments three weekends in a row just doesn't wash with many people.

"I don't know where my relationship with Tim will lead, but for now it is very special," she said.

Being a full-time university student, sometimes Cristina has to study for an exam and coach a tournament at the same time, which is quite a challenge! The State Floor Hockey Tournament in Anaheim was one such occasion.

With a physics final the following week, Cristina sat with her athletes and studied as the other games were played. One of her athletes, Joey, was very curious. "Cristina, watcha readin'; read to me, will ya," he goaded. Joey is a pudgy, Down syndrome fellow with a cheerful disposition. He carries a clipboard with various papers attached to it. With his ball cap perched on his head, he looks so official that oftentimes strangers will approach him to ask questions, to which he gives a happy grin.

"Okay, you asked for it!" she replied and then proceeded to read to him from her physics book. Later, Cristina set the book and papers on the floor and crossed the room to talk with one of the other coaches. When she returned, her notes were missing!

Frantically she searched for Joey. Upon finding him, she screeched, "Joey, have you seen my notes?"

"We must learn to feel comfortable in a world with people who are handicapped in some way, and I believe it is happening. I am confident my generation will teach our children that these are people just like us, worthy of love and respect."

"No, I didn't see your notes!" exclaimed Joey innocently.

Panic-stricken, she ran around asking everyone if they had seen her papers and notes. After what seemed an eternity, and with visions of an F in physics running through her mind, she heard her name over the loudspeaker. Racing to the paging area, she ran headlong into a coach who held her papers, now wadded in a crumpled mess. He smiled rather sheepishly and said, "I saw Joey throw these papers in the trash. Looks like they're your notes."

Weak with relief but very irritated, she marched over to Joey and shook the wrinkled papers in front of him. "Joey, I want you to promise me you will never, never take my notes again!"

Hanging his head in shame, he said, "I'm sorry, Cristina, I promise I'll never do it again."

"I melted at his contriteness," Cristina confessed, "and now before every practice, he says, 'Cristina, I promise I won't take your notes anymore.'

"Sometimes when I am in the library studying and bone tired," Cristina reflected, "I think, 'I don't want to do this anymore; I'm tired of the whole thing.' But I stop in the middle of my pity party and think of my athletes and realize how lucky I am to be able to study and work. I think of the effort they put forth, how they try and try; and I know I can't quit.

"Every day in my classes I hear people grumble about their lives and their problems. I wish I could take them to a Special Olympics tournament and say, 'Now complain!' "

When Cristina first started college, money was her main goal. "I wanted an education so I could be rich," she confessed.

This past year she made the profound discovery that there are more important ways to be rich than having a lot of money.

Cristina reflected on a recent basketball practice and on Jerry Phillips, a very low-functioning individual. Lost in his own world, Jerry normally pays no attention to what is happening around him. Cristina routinely made an extra effort to spend time talking to him, one-on-one. Until this particular evening he had never shown any recognition of her.

"Normally, before practice begins, we have free-throw time," she said. "When I took the ball to him and said, 'Jerry, shoot me a basket,' he looked me right in the eyes and took the ball. My heart made an extra beat as he walked over to the basket. First he dribbled the ball. Then he bent over, placed the ball between his legs, and with all his power, he thrust the ball and stood watching as it sailed up and curved back down landing solidly in the basket.

"Excitedly, I screamed, 'Jerry, you did it! You did it!'

"Clapping his hands he looked at me and yelled, 'Yea, Yea!'

"For a few moments, all other activity halted as I eagerly fed Jerry the balls, and one after another he shot baskets. Sometimes he made them, sometimes he didn't. But he was with us."

At the end of the evening when his foster mother came to pick him up, Cristina rushed up to her and exclaimed, "Sandy, you'll never believe what happened!" and she recounted the marvelous breakthrough. Jerry's mom watched him in action and could hardly believe her eyes.

One of the other coaches came over and patted Cristina on the back and said, "It's the coaching. It's the coaching."

"I guess I really want to believe it is the coaching," said Cristina, "and that I have made a difference in a life. It inspires me to want to do more and work harder for all the kids. Believe me, as I walked out of the gym that evening, I truly felt rich."

There was, however, one occasion when she felt like a green, wadded up dollar bill. It was at the Anaheim games. An exciting day at Disneyland was planned for all the athletes and coaches. Cristina's group consisted of herself, Head Coach Clara Downes, two other coaches, and eleven athletes.

As the day progressed, everyone was having a wonderful time on the rides, eating, and people watching. After several hours, it was time for a routine head count. Cristina recalled grimly, "I counted heads—ten. I counted again—ten. I counted again. There was no way I could come up with eleven. With my heart in my throat, I began calling off names and discovered that Richard was missing.

"Richard is a short, innocent looking young man who is thirty years old. Completely nonverbal and quite low functioning, he has little ability to care for himself.

"Trying not to panic, I calmly stated to the other coaches, 'I'm sure he is at the lost and found. You stay right here and I'll be back!' With that I gave rein to my panic and bolted as fast as my legs would carry me to the lost and found. No Richard!

" 'Oh, dear Lord, help,' I prayed. The crowds were one solid mass. Continually straining my eyes in every direction, I hurried back to the group.

"For two hours, we allowed the other athletes to enjoy the rides while I ran back and forth to the lost and found. The knot in my throat was so big that I could hardly swallow. Clearly, I didn't know what to do.

"As the evening drew to a close, we decided to take our group to the exits and watch for Richard. Finally, we spotted a family casually walking down the center of Main Street; Richard was with them. 'Richard, Richard!' Clara and I screamed as we ran up and threw our arms around him. I didn't know whether to hug the family or attack them for having him with them.

"When asked how they happened to have Richard, this Canadian girl said, 'We observed this young man riding the teacups time after time, and it didn't appear that he was with anyone. We could see he had a problem, so we decided to keep him with us until someone found him.'

"Richard stood there smiling at all of us as we tried to sort through what had happened. The family felt they did what was best in the situation, but I couldn't understand why they didn't take him to lost and found. Nevertheless, I expressed our profound thanks.

"Walking a few steps away, the family turned around and waved good-bye to Richard. He gave them a thumbs-up. As he turned back to us, a single tear ran down his cheek. I like to think it was because he was so glad to find us. I was so relieved, I could have watered a crop with my own tears!

"I would never have survived that ordeal had it not been for veteran coach Clara Downes, who encouraged me through the long hours. Anytime I plan to lose an athlete at Disneyland, I want to make sure she is right by my side," Cristina said with a grin.

Most of Cristina's involvement is not as dramatic as that just described. Sometimes it is just plain hard work. But the rewards always outweigh the labor. While, oftentimes, she goes home physically exhausted, mentally she is so wired that it takes several hours of talking and recounting with her family and friends before she can relax enough to fall asleep. The next day she is anxious to begin again.

Carolyn, her mother, is very supportive of her use of time and energy on behalf of Special Olympics. Cristina smiled and said, "Oh, she worries about how tired I sometimes get, but she is impressed with the changes in me. She has come to the tournaments and now knows the athletes I talk about so much."

Some interesting things about Cris's personality have come to light this past year. With newfound wisdom she says, "I enjoy life so much more today than I did a year ago. I have learned I have three times more patience than I ever thought I had. I have also learned I am a pretty good athlete. I never tried before.

"Life has never been better or fuller. My days start at six in the morning and are filled with school, a part-time job, Special Olympics, and Tim, when I can squeeze him in. I get home at ten at night. We coaches even have a soccer team of our own. We meet and play together once a week.

"What Special Olympics brings to me is unbelievable. Just because the athletes have mental retardation doesn't mean they can't live full lives. The energy they put into life is such an inspiration—they expend three times the amount of effort that I do.

"I hope that eventually society won't be uncomfortable with people with mental retardation. It hurts me to see people cross over to the opposite side of the street to keep from walking by them or moving to the next aisle at the grocery store. With love and education that can change.

"We must learn to feel comfortable in a world with people who are handicapped in some way, and I believe it is happening. I am confident my generation will teach our children that these are people just like us, worthy of love and respect.

"Special Olympics has gripped my life and I never plan to wrestle free."

Author's Note:

Cristina is my son Joel's floor hockey and basketball coach. It has been such a joy to watch her in action.

At a recent basketball tournament, during the warm-up period, all the members of her team were lined up to shoot baskets. Joel's turn came and Cristina quickly pulled a chair up under the basket. She stood on it and held her arms out in a big circle. Joel, who probably could never make a real basket, now had an attainable goal, a living basket.

Life is made up, not of great sacrifices or duties, but of little things, in which smiles and kindnesses and small obligations, given habitually, are what win and preserve the heart and secure comfort.

—Sir Humphry Davy

Our greatest danger in life is in permitting the urgent things to crowd out the important.

—Charles E. Hummel

Timothy Patrick Daly

"I could never give up what I have received from my athletes. They have given me so much love and have been so committed."

Timothy Patrick Daly

Timothy Patrick Daly is a financial analyst for HomeFed Bank in San Diego, California. His involvement with people with mental retardation began in Santa Barbara when, as a young boy, his mother's service club included in their charities a home for the cerebral palsied. Never having enough volunteers available, Tim was drafted into service.

"SKY BLUE DUVAL WAS A handful, and he was my baptism into Special Olympics," said Tim. "Today, after six years, the thought of him still warms my heart."

At the outset of that first weekend event, Tim had wondered why he had been assigned to such a small group. It didn't seem fair that the other coaches had so many to look after and he had only a couple of athletes. One hour with Sky Blue changed Tim's mind.

Very low-functioning, with no speech, Sky required constant supervision. His only event for that weekend was the Frisbee Toss. In the interim, Tim had to do everything for him: cut up his food, dress him, take him to the bathroom, and, most importantly, keep him away from anything glass—which he loved to break! It was physically and mentally challenging, but Tim found the weekend immensely enjoyable.

Tim's dark eyes reveal the emotion and sensitivity required of one gifted in working with those who are mentally retarded. A young man of quiet strength and ample patience, he smiles as he continues, "My parents came down from Santa Barbara to see me work at that first weekend event. They were as touched by Sky Blue Duval as I was.

"My mom said she could tell that Sky really thought a lot of me. Her years of working with retarded children have given her the ability to see and feel beyond the lack of words or communication.

"By Sunday I was so worn out that when a whole family, who were volunteering together, came up and asked if they could help, I gratefully relinquished Sky into their hands for a few hours. I had learned the hard way that it takes a whole family to watch him. However, I came away totally invigorated by the work."

Tim's last five years in Special Olympics have been as head coach in all sports. Single and committed to his job as a financial analyst by day, his nights belong to Special Olympics. His willingness to work where needed has put him in great demand throughout the organization.

Summer vacations are spent working sports camps for the state Special Olympics organization.

"I believe I have a God-given ability to work and interact with these people," said Tim. "It is my feeling that this is why I was put on this earth. However, I get so much pleasure in return that sometimes I feel rather selfish about the whole thing.

"My involvement has caused some problems with my parents," he continued. "They think I overdo it, and that the organization might be taking advantage of my willingness. Their concern is that I don't have any social life outside of Special Olympics, and that is true. What they don't realize is that I have made wonderful friends within the organization. We enjoy being together. We share common goals. We talk the same language. How much more social life do I need?

"I think my parents' main concern was that I didn't have a girlfriend. I have always known that whoever I became romantically involved with would have to be in Special Olympics or be very understanding of my involvement, because I never plan to give it up.

"One day, there she was, Cristina Henderson. I didn't even have to go looking for her! She is as committed to Special Olympics as I, and we share so much together. I never realized just how wonderful it would

"The people I have worked with in Special Olympics have helped me grow mentally, spiritually, and socially. It always amazes me how I became a coach. I was never really involved in sports; now it means so much to me."

be to have someone to share this work with. I think my parents are happy now. At least they have quit bugging me about doing too much."

Tim's involvement takes two or three evenings of his week and almost every weekend. In 1989 he was selected to be a state chaperone to the International Winter Games, which are held every four years. This particular year the Games were held in Nevada. Tim picked up his two ski athletes at the Los Angeles airport—Matt Kiker from Long Beach and Doris Davis from Antelope Valley—and they flew the rest of the trip together.

Both Matt and Doris are medium-functioning athletes, with Matt requiring more assistance than Doris. Matt tried so hard in the ski competition. He was a real fun-loving guy who wanted to do well. However, he was placed in the wrong category, and the slopes were too steep, so every two seconds he fell down.

"I constantly dashed across the snowy slopes to pick him up, brush him off, and give him some encouragement," said Tim. "He was the last athlete to come in, but he finally did cross the finish line. He was so excited. He kept yelling, 'Tim, I won! I won!' I never get over the joy of seeing the athletes' thrill of accomplishment."

"Doris was more accomplished in the novice division and didn't need as much help, but by the third day she was totally exhausted. The pace was grueling. We worked practically around the clock: up by 5:00 A.M., breakfast at 6:00, to the bus by 7:00, and on the slopes by 9:00. We were there until 4:00 P.M., then back for the evening event.

"I was originally slated to be the head coach for the Nordic Skiing, but because I only have two weeks' vacation from the bank, I can't take time off to devote to the event. I normally spend my vacation at Sports Camp or tournaments. Sometimes it's difficult to keep motivated and going, because I don't have time for myself. It would be nice now and then to have a 'vacation,' to step back and just relax. But I can't let my mother hear me say that!" Tim said with a laugh.

Tim has been approached about working for Special Olympics in a professional capacity as assistant area director and has seriously considered it. "It would mean a reduction in my income," he said, "but I personally feel one must love what he does for a living. So the reduction in wages wouldn't bother me that much. There may come a time when I do become a professional part of Special Olympics. I can't think of anything I would rather do as my life's work.

"The people I have worked with in Special Olympics have helped me grow mentally, spiritually, and socially. It always amazes me how I became a coach. I was never really involved in sports; now it means so much to me.

"I have worked with athletes in a wide range of ability levels, from extremely low- to high-functioning. I love working with them all. I also enjoy working with the wheelchair athletes.

"On one end of the spectrum, I work more with the athletes with their physical needs—wiping noses, dressing and undressing them, taking them out of their wheelchairs and placing them on the toilets. On the other end of the spectrum, I help the athletes cope with their frustrations when faulty limbs won't do what the brain commands them to do.

"I could never give up what I have received from my athletes. They have given me so much love and have been so committed. I have learned from them how to deal successfully with my own everyday problems. Every chance I get, I challenge people to become exposed to these very special people. They have insights into life that the average person never seems to grasp. People with mental retardation give so much more than they get."

Author's Note:

I have learned that this remarkable young man, in addition to his work with Special Olympics, spends one evening a week at the San Diego Children's Convalescent Hospital rocking sick children and taking them on outings.

The only religion that will do anything toward enriching your life is the religion which inspires you to do something toward enriching the lives of others.

—Author Unknown

I shall pass through this world but once. If, therefore, there be any kindness I can show, or any good thing I can do, let me do it now; let me not defer it or neglect it, for I shall not pass this way again.

—De Grellet

Julie Bales

"It's a great feeling to see people try so hard and to give 100 percent."

Julie Bales

Julie Bales was named Missouri Special Olympics Coach of the Year for 1988. A teacher for the E. W. Thompson State School for the severely handicapped in Sedalia, Missouri, she and her husband, Bill, met through Special Olympics and are the parents of one son.

YOUNG, ENERGETIC, AND VIVACIOUS, JULIE Bales juggles her teaching position, her new son, her home, and her volunteer work with Special Olympics gingerly, with each coming up first in her life. Thankfully, her husband, Bill, is there to help keep the juggling balls all airborne at the same time.

Exposed to Special Olympics while she was a college senior, Julie knew immediately she wanted to be involved. The first thing she did upon squaring away her new teaching position was to investigate the Special Olympics organization in Sedalia, Missouri. That first phone call introduced her to the man who was to become her husband.

Julie is now an eight-year veteran and has served a five-county area as chairman for the past four years. As is the case with most Special Olympics volunteers, Julie finds herself bathing athletes, feeding them, organizing meets, speaking to service clubs, and wiping runny noses, plus coaching skiing, basketball, bowling, track, soccer, and swimming.

Attendance at her first International Games, which were held in Baton Rouge, Louisiana, interrupted her honeymoon, but was nonetheless a highlight in her life, as she observed athletes from all around the world competing for the coveted gold and silver medals.

When asked about her favorite challenges with her athletes, she quickly recalled, "In 1985, Bill and I worked hard trying to prepare Mike, a nonverbal athlete, for that year's International Winter Games in Park City, Utah. Training an athlete for cross-country skiing, with as little snow as we have in Missouri, was no easy task. All of the practice had been on dry land. Mike practiced hard, three times a week, and he had done pretty well considering that only a few short weeks before he had never been on skis.

"We desperately wanted to see how he would do in snow. Early one evening snow flurries began to fall. By 10:00 P.M., there was enough snow on the ground to work with him. Knowing better than to wait until morning when the snow would be gone, I ran to the phone and called his mom. 'Dress him warm,' I told her. 'We're going to hit the closest slope we can find.'

"We sped to his house, banged on the door, grabbed him and his ski clothes, and drove like mad to a snowy spot where he got the much needed actual snow practice.

"A few weeks later Mike proudly brought back two silver medals from the Park City event."

The athletes are ingenious at making themselves understood. While at Park City, Julie and Mike were walking down the street when they passed a man Mike recognized as Darren of the television show, "Bewitched."

"Grabbing my sleeve, Mike pointed emphatically at the man who had just passed, and wiggled his nose furiously." Laughing, Julie continued, "I had no trouble figuring out what Mike was saying and we ran down the street after him. 'Darren, Darren, could we please have your autograph?' I hollered breathlessly as we ran to catch up with him. He smiled broadly and said, 'Sure!'

"He was also nice enough to allow us to take lots of pictures of Mike and him together. Mike's favorite pastime now is cornering anyone he can to show off his pictures with Darren."

Julie has discovered that some of her athletes have

"I have seen very shy, introverted individuals change, almost before my eyes, as Special Olympics helped them reach out and find themselves."

remarkable recall. Their minds are able to grasp and hold onto the past far more readily than most people realize. While in Baton Rouge for the International Swim Competition, Chris sat on a bench awaiting his event. He nervously wrapped his hands round and round a towel, continually bouncing his legs. Julie went over to him and wrapped him in a bear hug saying, "Come on, Chris, don't be so nervous; you're going to do great."

He replied haltingly, "Yes, that's right. All I hav'ta 'member is what Kim told me."

Kim had been Chris's swim teacher earlier in the year and had worked with Chris several times a week during that time period. Julie thought, *How great that Chris is now ready for competition and remembers what Kim told him.*

The things Kim taught Chris did work for him; he won a gold! When they returned home, Julie sought out Kim and shared what had transpired; Kim was happy to know that his efforts, months before, had made a difference.

"I have seen very shy, introverted individuals change, almost before my eyes, as Special Olympics helped them reach out and find themselves," Julie says.

One such person was Alisa. The school's speech therapist and Julie decided it was time to enlist a drill team and cheerleaders for the Special Olympics events.

Alisa, a very quiet, nonverbal, 10-year-old came to mind. They approached her apprehensive parents with the idea and, after a sell-job by the teachers, the parents agreed to give it a try, thinking full well it wouldn't work.

After three or four months of practice, the first competition was to be held on a Friday and Saturday, several miles from home. Alisa's parents agreed for her to go with the group to spend the first night but planned to be at the competition the following day and would drive her home.

The first night at the motel everyone prepared for bed. "Alisa was to sleep in the room with another coach and me," said Julie. "The rest of the girls were in an adjoining room. Alisa has an aversion to beds, so a pallet was made for her on the floor. The girls were all giggling and talking girl talk, but finally the time came to settle them down. 'Come on, Alisa, it's time to go to bed,' I said."

Alisa began fussing the minute she entered the room where she was to sleep. She immediately grabbed her pallet and, without the aid of her walker, hopped back to the room with the other girls. She was not going to miss out on being with the others.

Julie gave her assistant a quizzical look and exclaimed, "Is this the same shy, introverted little girl of three months ago?"

"We happily made her a pallet in the room with the other girls," said Julie.

"The next day at the competition Alisa did an exceptional job. She was so excited about her performance, and the fact that her parents were there to see her made it even better. As planned, after the competition her parents said, 'Okay, Alisa, let's go home.' Alisa immediately began to cry, indicating her desire to stay, which was a first for her and her parents. Normally she wouldn't have wanted her parents to leave her; now the situation was reversed.

"She is welcome to stay. There's a dance tonight, and she's been having a wonderful time," Julie informed the parents, pleadingly.

Reluctantly the parents agreed and left the field arm-in-arm, with one last backward glance for reassurance.

"Special Olympics athletes are a labor of love," says Julie, "and my niche in life is to work with them. They are my husband's and my friends. They visit our home and sometimes even spend the holidays with us. It's a great feeling to see people try so hard and to give 100 percent. Most so-called normal people don't do that."

Julie and Bill feel they are a part of an organization that is doing something great for others. They are already talking about the time when their small son will take his place with them in Special Olympics. "In a couple of years, he will be learning about and interacting with our special friends. Ours is a family affair!"

No man is born into the world whose work is not born with him. There is always work, and tools to work withal, for those who will.

—James Russell Lowell

Whatever God gives you to do, do it as well as you can. This is the best possible preparation for what He may want you to do next.

—George Macdonald

Bruce Harrison

"My life is filled with such joy...
of seeing athletes walk with their
heads high, proud of what they
have accomplished."

Bruce Harrison

Bruce Harrison is an adapted physical education teacher for the trainable and severely mentally impaired at Woodland Development Center in Marysville, Michigan. A recipient of the 1986 Michigan Special Olympics Coach of the Year Award, Bruce has been a volunteer since 1973 and currently serves as coordinator for St. Clair County. He and his wife, Martine, are the parents of three daughters, Jennifer, Kelly, and Megan.

BRUCE'S FIRST EXPOSURE TO SPECIAL Olympics came soon after he secured his first job as a teacher for the mentally impaired in Wayne County in the inner city of Detroit. He and good friend Andy Farrar realized that their students needed some type of athletic competition. With great ingenuity, they lined a three-lane track in a debris-filled playground using a bag of lime and a bent coffee can, so they could have their own local Special Olympics meet.

Bruce grew up with athletics and knew how important the competition had been in his own development, both in the pride of accomplishment and the self-esteem it brought him. He and Andy envisioned what an impact this could have on these largely forgotten, inner-city students.

Bingo! When the awards were handed out after that first meet, and Bruce and Andy saw the incredible pride written all over the faces of these young people and their parents, they were hooked. Bruce remembers, "It was then that I truly realized that I could be a provider of those emotions to a group of people who had never experienced them before. The joy continues. I am just as excited about my athletes and their events today as I was in 1973."

Special Olympics is continually on Bruce Harrison's mind, from September to June. He takes the summer months off to regroup and get reacquainted with his family.

"I don't think of myself as a volunteer," said Bruce. "I think of Special Olympics as my second job. It doesn't pay the bills or put food on my table, but still it is my second job. At school I am known as Coach and that is what I do, from the time we drop our first soccer ball at the start of the fall season until the last athlete has competed at the State Summer Games."

It is what Bruce and his massive force of volunteers do during that time that makes the various Special Olympics programs successful. This includes the upkeep and preparation of equipment and the filling out of registration forms. "No matter how long I have been doing the forms, it is still a battle to get them to the post office 15 minutes before registration deadline," he said with a grimace.

Countless contacts must be made in the transportation of athletes, scheduling of practices, securing of facilities, getting athletes ready to perform at their best, and the raising of funds to pay for the whole program. All of this takes many people, who become close friends as they share their commitment to the program.

Bruce's athletic physique belies his tenderness for his athletes and those responsible for their successes. "Grandma Holly is my foster grandmother," said Bruce, "and an important member of our Special Olympics team. She can be feisty at times, but I would be lost without her help in laundering uniforms and making sure they fit the athletes and in filling out ribbons for local events.

"My codirector, Maggie Dekoyer, along with Jim Demeester and Chuck Burge are totally dedicated. Their only goal is to provide opportunities for the special individuals we work with."

Each event has its own memory and place in

"To see the incredible determination of these athletes coupled with their joy of accomplishment, and to see the huggers at the finish line and the emotion in the faces of the crowd is absolutely matchless."

Bruce's heart. "No matter if we win or lose, they are all special in their own way," he said with a smile.

The Michigan State Soccer Tournament in 1985 was one such event. Brian was a team member who had been born with large webbed hands and feet. Called "thunder foot" because of the abnormal size of his shoes and his ability to kick the soccer ball extremely long distances, Brian was a different sort. An individual who would rather listen to rock music than breathe, everyone enjoyed him.

He played left defense in the semifinal game that year. The score was 0-0 and the game had just gone into its second overtime when Brian's goalie kicked the ball. It ricocheted off a defending player and came right to Brian. He whirled around and with his thunderous foot, drilled it high up into the right-hand corner of his own team's net for the winning goal—for the other team.

"Brian's first reaction was of incredible jubilation; mine was close to panic," Bruce recalled.

"We stood there, stunned, while Brian reveled in what he thought he had accomplished. A couple of the higher-functioning players finally told him what he had done, but it still didn't take away from his jubilation.

"After several moments I went up to him and tried to calmly explain that he had won the game for the other team. I encouraged him to try a little harder to shoot the ball the other way."

Bruce's deflation at losing that soccer match was quickly erased by the bronze medal won by his other athletes in another event.

The Winter Games of 1983 were to be held at Sugar Loaf Mountain in Traverse City, Michigan. Bruce and his coaches always try to keep a quota of athletes in different events and decided they would enter a speed-skating event.

Early on in the season, staff had advised Bruce that there was a new, higher-functioning young woman who fit the bill as a speed skater. Although registrations had to be turned in, there was no ice on which to try her. So Bruce took her word that she could handle the event with no problem and sent in her registration.

A few weeks later a local pond froze over and Bruce took her out to the ice, where he laced her skates for her very expectantly. Immediately she went over on her ankles.

"Right then I knew we were in for trouble," sighed Bruce. "I continued trying to train her, to no avail. She just could not stay up on the blades."

She was included in the roster of athletes for the Winter Games, but Bruce was concerned, not only for her, but for the other athletes and coaches who don't like to be embarrassed. They try always to compete on a good scale.

Her event was scheduled. "I had only one alternative," said Bruce. "I purchased a couple of rolls of athletic tape. After breakfast, on the morning of the 30-meter sprint, I taped her ankles—tight! Then I quickly laced her into her skates.

"She competed in two events and was up on her blades the entire time, taking two silver medals. She was thrilled. I was personally delighted that gangrene hadn't set in, but we made it!"

In Bruce's earlier years with Special Olympics, while still in the inner city of Detroit, he had an athlete by the name of Sheila. At the time, this young woman was 17 years old. Normally she was a sweet, extremely shy, kitten-like individual. However, if you crossed her, she could be a wildcat.

"When you put a pair of tennis shoes on her feet and lined her up for a race, she became a jaguar," said Bruce. "She ran like the wind. In the years I coached her, she never lost a race.

"Halfway down the track she would be smiling big, just glad to be running. She was a joy to watch, running free. How proud she was when she was presented medal after medal.

"Sheila topped off her Special Olympics career in 1975 when, at the International Games, she became one the fastest known female Special Olympians in the world. She will always have a special place in my heart. I still miss her to this day."

At most meets, Bruce has a contingent of wheel-chair athletes. Some are outstanding and some labor in their attempts to compete.

"Wesley, a small young man with big bright teeth, has a smile that melts the hearts of everyone. At the beginning of his 25- and 75-meter races, he literally did wheelies and quickly won the heats. That was the high point.

"The low point was watching some of the other wheelchair athletes take two and a half to three min-utes to do what Wesley did in 20 seconds.

"Most of the wheelchair athletes have cerebral palsy and they labor to get their wheelchairs across the finish line. To see the incredible determination of these athletes coupled with their joy of accomplishment, and to see the huggers at the finish line and the emo-tion in the faces of the crowd is absolutely matchless. It's one of the moments that should be freeze-framed for history," said Bruce, with an obvious lump in his throat.

Then there was Keith. A heavyset fellow whose clothes never seemed to quite fit, he was entered in the 30-meter snowshoe race at the State Winter Games. When the race began, Keith started off well, but at 10 meters he tripped over one of his snowshoes and fell. As he proceeded to get up, his jeans slipped down over his behind. With determination, he finished the 30 meters with his jeans wrapped around his knees.

"It was a sight to behold," said Bruce, "Keith, smiling broadly, pulled up his jeans, tried to anchor them in place, and collected his ribbon. The whole scenario was uproariously funny but also very heartwarming. Finishing that race was more important to Keith than pulling up his pants. I was very proud of him."

When asked if there was a spiritual significance to his working with Special Olympics, Bruce replied, "I was brought up in the teachings of the Catholic Church and believe that it is important to help others. If emotion is a form of spiritual reasoning, then maybe that is what I have for what I do. Special Olympics has, from the time I started, been a definite love. You do not do it with your head; you do it with your heart.

"One of the great sayings of the organization is 'You get hooked on it,' because of the love that is always shown at the various events. The spiritual love I have for these individuals is why I do my professional job of teaching and why I do my second job of Special Olympics," said Bruce.

Mentally impaired individuals are, by law, educated in the state of Michigan until they are 26 years of age. Students and teachers are together as many as 10 years. "A great bond of friendship develops during the years, and there is a painful sense of loss when they are gone."

In 1986 Bruce was voted Michigan Special Olympics Coach of the year. "It was a pinnacle of all the years I have spent and the effort I have tried to put forth," said Bruce. This event was shared by his wife, Martine. "I'm thankful to Martine for placing Special Olympics events on our calendar first thing in the new year and planning the rest of our lives around it, for understanding when I have to leave her at home for nights on end as we prepare for a tournament, for being in the stands with our three children, cheering our athletes at the State meets; without her support and love and the encouragement of my friends, I would not have been able to accept that award.

"My life is filled with such joy, joy of seeing pride in the eyes of parents, an emotion many of these parents had long ago laid to rest, and the joy of seeing athletes walk with their heads high, proud of what they have accomplished.

"After a four-day event, my volunteers and I come away emotionally and physically drained from loving and caring and hoping and feeling the triumphs and defeats of our athletes. I experience these emotions at least five times a year. When I realize that sometimes people don't go through one emotional situation like that in their whole lifetime, I feel blessed beyond measure," concluded Bruce Harrison.

To Make This Life Worthwhile

May every soul that touches mine,
Be it the slightest contact,
Get therefrom some good;
Some little grace; one kindly thought;
One aspiration yet unfelt;
One bit of courage
For the darkening sky;
One gleam of faith
To brave the thickening ills of life;
One glimpse of brighter skies
Beyond the gathering mists,
To make this life worthwhile.

—George Eliot

Janet Sharp

"I wish with all my heart that the rest of the world could see and understand the hearts of these athletes so we could all be like them."

Janet Sharp

Janet Sharp is employed by Kew Cottages, an institution for the intellectually disabled in Melbourne, Australia, as the swimming instructor/pool manager. The 1988 recipient of the Australia Special Olympics Coach of the Year Award, Jan has won international acclaim for her work with the Halliwick Method of swimming. She presented a paper at Congress Halliwick at Nijmegen University, Holland, and has been informed that her paper is to be published as a reference work.

Jan smiled at the irony of a bad back having placed her at home on a beautiful Australian fall day, granting her the time to pause and reflect on her life with Special Olympics. Parrots and cockatoos outside her window chattered gaily and unfolded their brightly colored wings as they flew about.

"One of my memories is Phillip, a young lad who had a disability that would take his life at a very young age," Jan shared. "When he was introduced to Special Olympics, he was about 20 and already confined to a wheelchair. We searched for an event in which he could compete and finally settled on the tennis ball throw. After much frustration and practice, to his amazement and our joy, he took first place in this event at regional level. The regional committee then began plans for an awards supper/dance.

"Invitations were printed and sent out, catering was secured, and a band was hired. Then I received a phone call from Phillip's teacher asking if we could push the event forward as Phillip wasn't expected to live beyond a few weeks; they were afraid he would miss the ceremony. She said, 'Phillip is just living for that event. You have no idea what it means to him to be a winner.'

"I just went cold all over thinking that in a few short weeks this charming lad would die.

"I didn't quite know how we would go about rescheduling this event, but one thing was certain, we had to do it. Although the event wasn't as spectacular as we had first planned, we scurried around and the night finally came.

"Phillip was there all dressed up. He was very, very weak, but even in that condition he glowed with excitement. When his name was called to receive his certificate, someone wheeled him forward. To everyone's amazement, he then pushed himself up and stood with his head held high to accept his award. Those of us who knew his situation were overcome with emotion; there wasn't a dry eye in the place. Phillip's smile lit up our world—and keeps it lit. A few short weeks later, he was gone. But, oh, what a legacy he left behind!

"That isn't necessarily a happy story, but that's what Special Olympics is all about. To a healthy person, a ribbon or a certificate doesn't always mean much, but to the Phillips of this world Special Olympics means everything."

Janet Sharp was born of English parents; her father worked for the government on the Rock of Gibraltar. Physically disabled due to war injuries, Janet says of her father, "He was a wonderful fellow. Under his leadership, our family learned to work together. I'm sure he's the one who gave me the courage to go on with Special Olympics, because he had so much courage himself."

Janet, her husband, Jim, and their two adopted sons immigrated to Australia about 25 years ago, and shortly thereafter her name was "bobbed" to Jan by the Australians. Following their arrival, a son was born to the Sharp family. Now, the entire family, including their three sons and daughters-in-law, are involved in some way with Special Olympics. In 1990, the Sharp family received the Australia Special Olympic Award for the most outstanding family.

"To a healthy person, a ribbon or a certificate doesn't always mean much, but to the Phillips of this world Special Olympics means everything."

"My first exposure to intellectually disabled people was in 1974," said Janet. "While employed as a full-time coach at a successful swimming center, I read an advertisement in the paper asking for volunteers at Kew Cottages. I answered the ad and spent several frustrating weeks watching other volunteers fumble with trying to teach these people how to swim. I hadn't wanted to step on any toes by saying I was a qualified swimming instructor, but finally I got up the nerve. 'Please, just take over and help us,' they insisted. 'So I did.'"

Jan went from strength to strength at Kew Cottages, organizing programs, obtaining pool space and training volunteers. "The more involved I became with the disabled, the more disillusioned I grew with the regular coaching world—the poor sportsmanship, back-biting, etc. So when Kew Cottages built their own pool, I found myself employed full-time there. Kew Cottages is home to about 700 people ranging in age from 18 to 96 years, and I love them all."

Shortly after Jan began to work with the intellectually disabled, she attended a seminar on Sports for the Disabled where she was told that competition was not good for people who were intellectually disabled, because they were already failures and they could fail again.

"I was absolutely horrified at this philosophy," said Jan. "I had never thought of these people as failures.

They are some of the most courageous and gutsy people I have ever met!

"In 1975, I saw another advertisement in the paper, this one announcing a public meeting to introduce Special Olympics to Australia. I went to the meeting and have been involved in Special Olympics ever since.

"We faced a lot of opposition introducing Special Olympics into Australia, but it was an exciting time. Over 1000 people turned out for our first meeting, and Australia Special Olympics was born."

Jan sometimes finds it difficult to know where her job ends and Special Olympics begins. She is on the National Board of Directors and chairs the National Steering Committee for Public Education. She is the National Head Swimming Coach and at the state level Jan is the Director of Coaches Training, responsible for all coaches courses conducted in Victoria. She acts as advisor to Special Olympics International and the Australian Coaches Association. Regionally she coaches her own swimming squad.

In 1990, Special Olympics held their III National Games. Jan chaired "Sports Controllers Meetings" which were responsible for all sports conducted at the National Games.

Jan has traveled extensively on behalf of Special Olympics, attending International Games in America as their swimming coach, and going to the Asian Pacific Coaches and Directors Conference in Hong Kong as well as training sessions in Hawaii. "I've seen the Hong Kong Games and the Games in England," she said. "On a visit to Singapore I assisted by giving information on gymnastics and swimming sessions.

"While in Hawaii, I met a wonderful American gentleman and later, when my husband and I went back for a holiday, he and his family invited us to participate in their Thanksgiving celebration. What a treat to be accepted into this family and to be a part of this American tradition. Special Olympics has opened doors that would not have opened for us otherwise."

One of Jan's favorite stories is about Ashley, a physically fit young man with autistic tendencies who was preparing to go to America for the International Games. He had caused his parents some anxiety, as schools and sheltered workshops voiced concerns over his behavior. Nevertheless, he was a good swimmer and Jan wanted to take him as one of the four swimmers from Australia.

Now the athletes are expected to raise as much support as possible; Ashley was no exception. The little town where he lived got behind his efforts and before long he was washing windows and cars and mowing lawns. And the more he worked, the more confident he became.

Once in America, Ashley began to be aware of the "team." He began to relate and work with other people and soon he was accepted. Jan said, "Sometimes Ashley would come up to me and lightly touch my arm to let me know he was there. He never wanted to be touched, so I would nod to him that I understood."

He brought home a gold medal for the Australian Relay Team. That really clenched it for Ashley; he was a part of something. Fully aware that there were four people on the team, he was proud to be one of them.

Ashley's arrival in his hometown caused quite a stir, and he received a lot of publicity. He went back to school a changed young man, confident and sure of himself. Ashley's teachers marveled at the change and before long he was transferred to a workshop where he did extremely well. "The last I heard, Ashley was in open employment. He never looked back," said Jan with a smile.

Jan paused briefly and then went on to share about John, another swimmer.

"John and his 76-year-old father lived together (John's mother had died some years before). Early in his life, John was introduced to swimming by his father, a former swimmer himself. When competition time came around at the local swim club to which they belonged, John was always placed with the 10- and 11-year-old kids. A man of 28, he was intelligent enough to know he was swimming with the little ones.

"When John was introduced to Special Olympics, he was put in races with like swimmers. He immediately sped through the swimming events, winning meet after meet. In a short time, he was selected for the International Games Swim Team. His father was ecstatic and immediately asked to accompany the team to America. At this time it was not known that John's father had a serious health condition. The team and supporters were very concerned about him travelling the great distance to the U.S.A. But as we saw his excitement over his son representing Australia, we knew we could not have stopped him from making the trip."

While in America, the father got sick and spent about four days in the hospital. John's brother, who also went along, informed Jan that his dad was dying of cancer, but that his heart's desire was to see his son win a gold medal for Australia. He did see that and came home to live another five or six months.

"After the trip was over," said Jan, "and we were doing our recap of all that had transpired, each of the coaches was so glad that we had given John's dad this once-in-a-lifetime opportunity to see his son in such a winning position.

"If you had asked me before my involvement with

Special Olympics if I believed in God, I would probably have said no," related Jan. "But now when things
go wrong, I find myself praying to Him. I look out the
window and see all the beauty that surrounds us and
I know there must be a Superior Being who created it.
I see the love and goodness of the intellectually disabled;
I see their warmth and kindness. Going to the International Games in America both times, I experienced
how the Games touched us all. It was very spiritual.
All around us was love—in the brilliance of Special
Olympics, where people from all around the world were
together, all speaking different languages. We were all
there for one common cause, and we communicated
through the language of Special Olympics.

"At the International Games, as with any Special
Olympics Games, there is companionship, sportsmanship, and a sense of looking out for each other. I've
seen people barely able to manage a lunch tray for themselves, reaching out to help someone else. I've seen athletes stop during competition and help their opponent.

"I wish with all my heart that the rest of the
world could see and understand the hearts of these people, so we could all be like them.

"The feeling of well-being never leaves us once
we have seen the International Games. When we are
down and feel like the world is kicking us in the
teeth, all we have to do is look back and remember the

International Games. We've seen God at work. My question is why doesn't He do this for everyone—why for just a few of us? I guess we're the lucky ones."

Author's Note:

In June 1990, Jan Sharp was awarded the "Order of Australia Medal." This award is part of Australia's system of honors and awards established in 1975 by Her Majesty the Queen. Her Majesty, as Queen of Australia, is Sovereign Head of the Order and bestows the medal for service worthy of particular recognition.

Epilogue

When I began gathering the stories you have just read, my quest was to find the silver thread that binds these people and the other 500,000 Special Olympics volunteers they represent. What makes them do what they do? What makes them give so much of themselves year after year on behalf of my son and the nearly 1 million athletes with mental retardation who are involved in Special Olympics?

I found my answer, and it is a simple one: They receive much more than they give. They see courage and it becomes theirs; they see faith and it becomes theirs; they see joy and it becomes theirs. Above all, they see a special beauty of spirit and it becomes theirs.

Mary Francess Froese
May 1991

Glossary

Developmental disabilities

An "umbrella" term that includes all disabilities which cause substantial functional limitations in one or more of seven areas (learning, language, self-care, mobility, self-sufficiency, self-direction and independent living).

Persons with developmental disabilities living in the United States are estimated to be about 10 million. The most prevalent disabilities included in developmental disabilities are mental retardation, cerebral palsy, autism, head injury, and seizure disorders.

Mental retardation

One out of every 10 Americans has a person in his family with mental retardation—that's about 3% of our population or 7 million individuals. Mental retardation knows no race, religion, or nationality. It touches every educational, social, and economic background. Most (89%) have mild mental retardation who, with help, generally can achieve independence.

How are people with mental retardation different?

By definition, a person with mental retardation is one who, from childhood, develops at a below average rate and experiences difficulty in learning, social adjustment, and economic productivity.

Mild mental retardation

Persons with mild mental retardation differ from those without mental retardation only in rate and capacity of intellectual development. Their retardation is not usually apparent until they enter school.

Moderate mental retardation

Persons with moderate mental retardation usually show their developmental delay before reaching school age. Appropriate community-based education throughout their developmental years can prepare these people to live satisfying and productive lives.

Severe and profound mental retardation

Persons with severe and profound mental retardation have pronounced developmental problems and frequently have other disabilities in addition to mental retardation. Not too many years ago it was believed these persons were destined to a life of complete dependency and that they could not learn. However, systematic training efforts have proven that, with very few exceptions, persons with severe and profound retardation can learn to care for some of their basic needs. Many also can perform useful work activities, with supervision, and can otherwise adapt to normal patterns of life.

What causes mental retardation?

Any condition that hinders or interferes with intellectual development before or during birth or in the early childhood years can be the cause of mental retardation. Among the well-known causes are: German measles in the mother during the first three months of pregnancy, syphilis, meningitis, toxoplasmosis, Rh-factor incompatibility between the mother and infant, malnutrition and chromosome abnormalities, such as Down syndrome, which occurs in one out of 600 babies born. Drug and alcohol use during pregnancy are also significant contributing factors. The greatest causes of mental retardation are cultural familial factors. Organic causes like those listed above account for at most 20% of causes.

Can people with mental retardation become self-supportive?

Since most persons with mental retardation have mild mental retardation (89%), 75-percent, or three out of every four, can become self-supportive. Persons with mental retardation have been known to be highly motivated, hard-working employees. They rate tops in reliability, loyalty, accuracy, punctuality, and job satisfaction. They want to learn. They want to be useful. They want to become a part of the mainstream of humanity. However, most persons with moderate to profound mental retardation do not become self-supportive.

Down syndrome

Down syndrome is the most prevalent genetic condition associated with mental retardation. Approximately 5,000 such children are born each year. Down syndrome is a combination of birth defects that includes mental retardation. The degree of retardation varies widely from mild to severe. When the egg from the mother unites with the sperm from the father, this normally results in 23 chromosomes each from the mother and father and a baby is formed. Chromosomes are the hereditary information packets of every living cell. If 24 chromosomes are present (this is only one of three chromosomal abnormalities that produce Down syndrome), this causes the more than 50 clinical characteristics of Down syndrome.

Cerebral palsy

This is not a single disorder but a group of permanent disabling symptoms characterized by difficulty in muscular control and coordination. It is caused by damage to the part of the brain that controls and coordinates muscular action. Most often cerebral palsy occurs before, during, or immediately after birth because the supply of oxygen to the fetal or newborn brain is interrupted. It can also be caused from brain damage resulting from an accident, child abuse, or lead poisoning from swallowing bits of lead paint. Cerebral palsy ranges from only a slight awkwardness of gait to a severe loss of muscular control in several areas of the body. Some 700,000 persons in the United States are affected. It is estimated that each year 10,000 are born with cerebral palsy or acquire it early in life. Cerebral palsy does not necessarily mean that mental retardation is present as well.

Autism

Autism is a severely incapacitating, life-long developmental disability that usually appears during the first three years of life. Symptoms include a slow development or lack of physical, social, and learning skills; immature rhythms of speech, limited understanding of ideas, and use of words without attaching the usual meaning to them; abnormal responses to sensations—sight, hearing, touch, pain—and abnormal ways of relating to people, objects, or events.

Autism occurs either by itself or in association with other disorders that affect brain function. Prenatal viral infections, metabolic disturbances, seizure disorder, or mental retardation may result in autistic behavior. Autism may or may not be accompanied by mental retardation.

Seizure disorder

Seizure disorder (also known as epilepsy) is a condition that occurs when there are sudden, brief changes in how the brain works. One percent of the population, more than two million people, are now affected. A convulsive (grand mal) seizure happens when the whole brain is suddenly swamped with extra electrical energy. The body stiffens briefly and begins jerking movements. The tongue may be bitten. Breathing may become shallow. The jerking movements slow down after a few seconds and the seizure ends after a minute or two. After returning to consciousness, the person may feel confused and sleepy. In most cases people can go back to their normal activities after resting for a short period of time. A non-convulsive (petit mal) seizure happens when the extra brain activity stays in just one part of the brain. While the seizure is happening, the person looks as if he were in a trance. This usually lasts for only a few seconds, during which the person appears to be staring or blacking out and may blink or experience chewing movements. Some people who experience seizure disorders do so in response to flickering lights, seeing the sun flicker through the trees, or the rolling of a television screen. People with seizure disorders have dozens of seizures in their lives without noticeable changes in intelligence or alertness.

Facts About Special Olympics and How You Can Get Involved

Special Olympics
an international program of
year-round training and athletic competition for all
children and adults with mental retardation.

Special Olympics Oath
Let me win,
but if I cannot win,
let me be brave in the attempt.

Eunice Kennedy Shriver, Founder and Honorary Chairman
Sargent Shriver, Chairman of the Board
Douglas W. Single, President and Chief Executive Officer

Facts About Special Olympics and How You Can Get Involved

Introduction

Since 1968, millions of individuals with mental retardation have participated in Special Olympics. Currently, nearly one million athletes from ages eight to over eighty participate in programs in more than eighty countries.

Special Olympics is an international movement, adapting to the cultural and social structures of countries on every continent. The program transcends barriers of politics, economics, religion and language to unite the United States and the Soviet Union, Poland and Cuba, Northern and Southern Ireland, Israel and Jordan, Nepal and Nicaragua under the Special Olympics flag.

Special Olympics has earned the support of prominent world leaders ranging from Pope John Paul II to

U.S. President George Bush and former President Ronald Reagan, to Premier Fidel Castro of Cuba, to former Prime Minister Margaret Thatcher of Great Britain, to Jordan's Queen Noor, to Lady Youde of Hong Kong, to Deng Pufang of China, to former Prime Minister Rajiv Ghandi of India.

Special Olympics is endorsed by the international governing bodies of its 22 sports. Special Olympics also has been recognized and endorsed by the International Olympic Committee (IOC). This endorsement grants Special Olympics the right to use the Olympic name worldwide.

Special Olympics is administered almost entirely by more than 500,000 volunteers of all ages and backgrounds worldwide. It is one of the most successful sports organizations in the world in attracting and using volunteers to administer its day-to-day programs. Volunteers include students, senior citizens, members of civic and fraternal groups, amateur and professional athletes, sports officials and coaches, teachers, parents, business people and many more.

Special Olympics is a celebration of spirit, an occasion for joy and a beacon of hope for individuals with mental retardation and their families. It enables the athletes, their families and friends, volunteers and spectators to see and understand the true potential of every human being. It salutes the athletes' skill, their courage and their spirit, setting a world stage for all to see their triumphs over tremendous obstacles.

History

The concept of Special Olympics began in the early 1960s when Eunice Kennedy Shriver started a daycamp for people with mental retardation. From that experience, it was clear that people with mental retardation were far more capable in sports and physical activities than many experts believed. In 1968, Mrs. Shriver organized the First International Special Olympics Games held at Soldier Field, Chicago, Illinois, USA. Special Olympics was officially recognized and endorsed by the International Olympic Committee in an historic agreement signed on February 15, 1988. It is the only organization authorized by the IOC to use "Olympics" on a worldwide basis. Since its founding in 1968, millions of children and adults with mental retardation have participated in Special Olympics.

Mission

The mission of Special Olympics International, Inc., is to provide year-round sports training and athletic competition in a variety of Olympic-type sports for all children and adults with mental retardation, giving them continuing opportunities to develop physical fitness, demonstrate courage, experience joy and participate in the sharing of gifts, skills and friendship with their families, other Special Olympics athletes and the community.

Goal

To help bring all persons with mental retardation into the larger society under conditions whereby they are accepted, respected and given the chance to become useful and productive citizens.

Philosophy

Special Olympics is founded on the belief that people with mental retardation can, with proper instruction and encouragement, learn, enjoy and benefit from participation in individual and team sports, adapted as necessary to meet the needs of those with special mental and physical limitations.

Special Olympics believes that consistent training is essential to the development of sports skills and that competition among those of equal abilities is the most appropriate means of testing these skills, measuring progress and providing incentives for personal growth.

Special Olympics believes that through sports training and competition, people with mental retardation benefit physically, mentally, socially and spiritually; families are strengthened; and the community at large, both through participation and observation, is united in understanding people with mental retardation in an environment of equality, respect and acceptance.

The Spirit of Special Olympics—skill, courage, sharing and joy—incorporates universal values which transcend all boundaries of geography, nationality, political philosophy, gender, age, race, or religion.

Principles

To provide the most enjoyable, beneficial and challenging activities for athletes with mental retardation, Special Olympics operates worldwide in accordance with the following principles and beliefs.

- That, as a means of achieving this goal, Special Olympics encourages its more capable athletes to move from Special Olympics training and competition into school and community programs where they can train and compete in regular sports activities. The athletes may, at this point, wish to leave Special Olympics or continue to take part in Special Olympics activities. The decision is the athlete's.
- That all Special Olympics activities—at the local, state, national and international level—reflect the values, standards, traditions, ceremonies and events embodied in the modern Olympic movement, broadened and enriched to celebrate the moral and spiritual qualities of persons with men-

tal retardation so as to enhance their dignity and self-esteem.

• That participation in Special Olympics training programs and competitive events is open to all people with mental retardation who are at least eight years old, regardless of the degree of their disability.

• That comprehensive, year-round sports training is available to every Special Olympics athlete, conducted by well-qualified coaches in accordance with the standardized Sports Rules formulated and adopted by Special Olympics International; and that every athlete who participates in a Special Olympics sport will have been trained in that sport.

• That every Special Olympics program includes sports events and activities that are appropriate to the age and ability of each athlete, from motor activities to the most advanced competition.

• That Special Olympics provides full participation for every athlete regardless of economic circumstance and conducts training and competition under the most favorable conditions possible, including facilities, administration, training, coaching, officiating and events.

- That Special Olympics gives each participant an equal chance to excel by basing competition in every event on accurate records of previous performance or trial heats and, when relevant, grouping by age and gender.
- That, at every Awards Ceremony, in addition to the traditional medals for first, second and third places, athletes finishing from fourth to last place are presented a suitable place ribbon with appropriate ceremony.
- That, to the greatest extent possible, Special Olympics activities will be run by and involve local volunteers, from school and college age to senior citizens, in order to create greater opportunities for public understanding of and participation with people with mental retardation.
- That, although Special Olympics is primarily and essentially a program of sports training and competition, efforts are made to offer, as an integral part of Special Olympics Games, a full range of artistic, social and cultural experiences such as dances, art exhibits, concerts, visits to historic sites, clinics, theatrical and motion picture performances and similar activities.
- That the goal of Special Olympics in every nation is to develop organizations and conduct events at the community level. Countries which,

because of specific economic, social or cultural circumstances, may find it difficult to achieve this goal rapidly, may hold National Games on a regular basis to enhance the development of popular understanding and provide increased visibility for their citizens with mental retardation. All participating countries are invited to send a delegation to the International Games held every two years, alternating between Summer and Winter, provided that, in all cases Special Olympics standards are adhered to in the preparation of athletes and coaches for the Games.

• That the families of Special Olympics athletes are encouraged to play an active role in their community Special Olympics program, to share in the training of their athletes and to assist in the public education effort needed to create greater understanding of the emotional, physical, social and spiritual needs of people with mental retardation and their families.

• That Special Olympics encourages community, state and national sports programs, both professional and amateur, to include demonstrations by Special Olympics athletes as part of their major events.

• That Special Olympics activities take place in public, with full coverage by the media, so that athletes with mental retardation may reveal to the world those special qualities of the human spirit in which they excel—skill, courage, sharing and joy.

Benefits

Special Olympics contributes to the physical, social and psychological development of people with mental retardation. Through sports, athletes gain confidence and build a positive self-image which carries over into the classroom, home, job, and community. Involvement in Special Olympics also strengthens families, causing a richer appreciation of talents and greater support between the athlete, parents, siblings, relatives and guardians. Special Olympics fosters friendships between volunteers and athletes and provides a forum for better understanding of the capabilities of people with mental retardation.

Eligibility

Eligible for participation in Special Olympics are those individuals at least eight years old who are identified by an agency or professional as having mental retardation or have cognitive delays as measured by formal assessment or have significant learning or vocational problems due to cognitive delay which require or have required specifically designed instruction.

Sports

Sports are the vehicle used by Special Olympics to enrich the lives of individuals with mental retardation for two major reasons. The first is the physical and mental benefits of sports training and competition. Secondly, sports are larger than life, a mirror of life, and a means to help persons with mental retardation participate more fully in life. Athletic competition is a focal point in the lives of millions of people around the world. The aspirations and accomplishments of teams or individuals are a source of personal and national pride. Further, there is perhaps no better symbol of mankind's quest for excellence. Through discipline, dedication and commitment, people reach for and achieve their true potential, running faster, jumping higher, becoming stronger. Special Olympics offers training and competition in 22 Olympic-type sports:

Official Summer	*Official Winter*	*Demonstration*
Aquatics	Alpine Skiing	Canoeing
Athletics	Figure Skating	Cycling
Basketball	Floor Hockey	Powerlifting
Bowling	Nordic Skiing	Table Tennis
Equestrian	Poly Hockey	Team Handball
Football (Soccer)	Speed Skating	Tennis
Gymnastics		
Roller Skating		
Softball		
Volleyball		

Competition Divisions

Special Olympics is unique among sports organizations. It accommodates competitors of all ability levels by assigning them to competition divisions based on scores in previous performances, age and gender. Every athlete has a fair and equal chance to win, and by doing his or her best against competitors of similar skill, athletes succeed whether they place first or last. Through the divisioning process, all athletes have an opportunity to advance to Chapter, National and International Games. All competitions follow the Official Special Olympics Sports Rules, which have been adapted from the official rules of the international governing body of each sport.

Training

Special Olympics is founded on the belief that quality training is crucial to success in sports. Training programs to improve athletes' overall fitness and sport-specific competence have been developed, tested and outlined in a Sports Skills Program Guide in each sport. Special Olympics is the only worldwide sports organization which produces and disseminates such guides. In addition, a Coaches Training and Certification program instructs coaches and officials in the most effective techniques for working with athletes with mental retardation. Special Olympics athletes are trained by over 140,000 qualified coaches.

Families

Special Olympics is also unique among sports organizations with the focus on family. The program enables a family to share new activities and interests with their athlete, while feeling pride in their athlete's achievements. Family members of athletes are encouraged to be involved with their athlete's training to maximize these benefits and increase the athlete's physical activity.

Games

Special Olympics athletes train year-round for sports competitions which are patterned after the Olympic Games. Over 15,000 Games, meets and tournaments are held each year in both summer and winter sports in communities worldwide. Chapter games are held annually and National programs hold Games on an annual or biennial basis. These culminate in the International Games every two years, alternating between winter and summer sports.

Governance

Special Olympics International guides local, county, state and national programs from its Washington D.C. headquarters.

International policies are determined by a volunteer Board of Directors comprised of business and government leaders, professional athletes, educators and experts in mental retardation from around the world.

Financial and Cooperative Support

Special Olympics organizations are supported by funds raised from individuals, organizations, corporations, foundations and other sources. SOI is supported by the National Governing Bodies and/or International Sports Federation of each sports organization and a host of world leaders.

Volunteers

More than 500,000 volunteers enable Special Olympics to offer sports training and competition programs to nearly one million individuals with mental retardation on a worldwide basis. Special Olympics would not exist—and indeed would not have been created—without the countless time, limitless energy, dedication and commitment of volunteers.

In addition to the critical role which volunteers play in conducting training and competition programs, they are also important to Special Olympics' goal of increasing opportunities for integration and socialization for individuals with mental retardation. The involvement of volunteers allows Special Olympics to provide mainstreaming experiences for its athletes.

Volunteers include students, senior citizens, business people, family members of athletes, amateur and professional athletes and coaches, teachers, and many others. They fill a wide variety of roles for Special Olympics programs at the local, state, national and international levels, from the role of coach, to timer and scorer.

International Programs

Around the world, there are accredited Special Olympics programs in over 80 countries and programs in development in more than 20 other nations.

U.S. Chapter Programs

In the U.S., Special Olympics programs take place in 25,000 communities within the framework of Chapters in 50 states, the District of Columbia and three territories. The primary goal of the U.S. program is to reach thousands more athletes through a "JOIN THE WORLD OF WINNERS" outreach campaign.

Model School District Programs are underway in U.S. Chapters to offer extra-curricular and interscholastic sports options to elementary and secondary students with mental retardation and to include Special Olympics in the physical education curriculum. Model Community programs coordinate Special Olympics training and competition in schools, community recreation programs, group homes, and institutions.

Special Olympics and Education

Sports play a major role in the lives of students, whether they are participating on the field of play or cheering from the grandstand. School physical education programs teach sports skills to students, who then have the opportunity to use these skills in intramural, interscholastic, community recreation and personal sports activities. However, for most students with mental retardation, the opportunity to participate in sports activities often remains unfulfilled because the additional training and competition opportunities needed to develop their skills are not available.

Together, Special Olympics and schools can provide additional training and competition opportunities through existing physical education and after school sports programs. Here students with mental retardation learn to play a sport properly and compete against their peers.

Special Olympics is a means to an end; not an end in itself. The ultimate goal is to assure that an appropriate sports training and competition program exists for all students with mental retardation.

Towards this end, Special Olympics has developed sports programs that specifically integrate students with mental retardation into existing school sports programs:

Partners Club

This program unites high school or college students with Special Olympics athletes in an environment that provides sports skills training and athletic competition on a regular basis, as well as opportunities to enjoy other social and recreation activities in the school and community (i.e., parties, dances, field trips).

The Partners Club is a sanctioned school club with a faculty advisor and officers who network with school administration, athletic and physical education departments. Club meeting frequency and format should follow normal school club policies and procedures. Members may include varsity or junior varsity athletes and students with a particular career or sport interest. The local Special Olympics program provides on-going technical assistance to ensure proper sports training for all.

Training

• All Partners attend Special Olympics training school.

- All Partners utilize *Special Olympics Sports Skills Guides* and skills assessments for training Special Olympics athletes.
- Each Partner coaches the same athlete for a minimum of eight weeks prior to the first level of competition in that sport.

Competition

- Partners plan and conduct Special Olympics mini–competitions prior to Special Olympics local competition.
- Partners attend Special Olympics local, area and state Special Olympics competitions to cheer for their team and serve as assistant coaches.
- Partners help plan and facilitate the transition of Special Olympics athletes from school to community sports and leisure activities.

School Sports Partnerships

The purpose of this program is to expand existing after–school sports programs to include training and competition for students with mental retardation in conjunction with interscholastic sports teams.

Training and competition are supervised in accordance with normal school policy and procedure by the school's head coach in a particular sport or an assistance coach specifically assigned to Special Olympics teams. Athletes without handicaps from varsity and junior varsity sports teams serve as peer coaches, scrimmage teammates and boosters during competition.

Training

- Integrate warm-up, cool-down and conditioning activities with varsity athletes.
- Practice skill development using a station format with peer coaching by varsity athletes where possible.
- Provide ample opportunities for a variety of scrimmages between Special Olympics athletes and varsity/junior varsity athletes; mixed teams of athletes drawn from all sports teams, and Special Olympics teams.

Competition

- Conduct competition among athletes with disabilities alongside existing interscholastic compeitions. For example, in a track and field meet, a varsity 100-meter dash is followed by a Special Olympics 100-meter dash. In distance races, all athletes start together. Meet scores are tabulated for varsity, Special Olympics and Partnership teams.
- Conduct Special Olympics competitions just prior to varsity or junior varsity competitions. For example, Special Olympics basketball games are played prior to and at the same site as the var-

sity or junior varsity game and against a team from the same school.

- Conduct a tournament for Special Olympics partnership teams in conjunction with varsity tournaments.

Unified Sports

Introduced in 1987 as a pioneer program, Unified Sports combines approximately equal numbers of athletes with and without mental retardation, of similar age and ability, on teams that compete against other Unified Sports teams. Unified Sports is an important program because it expands sports opportunities for athletes seeking new challenges and furthers the Special Olympics commitment to foster integration in school and community sports programs.

In 1989, after two years of field testing, the Unified Sports program was launched throughout the United States. Currently, Special Olympics Unified Sports are established in Basketball, Bowling, Distance Running, Football (Soccer), Softball and Volleyball. Pilot programs are under development in several more sports.

Unified Sports is a unique and important program because it:

- Integrates athletes with and without mental retardation in a setting where all athletes are challenged to improve their skills;
- Provides a valuable sports opportunity to individuals with mental retardation who are not presently involved with Special Olympics; especially those with mild retardation, and those in communities where there are not enough Special Olympics athletes to conduct team sports;
- Prepares athletes with higher level skills for participation in school or community sports;
- Increases public awareness of the spirit and skills of individuals with mental retardation;
- Enables Special Olympics athletes' families to participate as team members or coaches on Unified Sports teams;
- And enables athletes to develop friendships and an understanding of each other's capabilities through a spirit of equality and team unity.

A Special Olympics Unified Sports program can be conducted in a variety of settings, including:

- A program organized by a Special Olympics group;
- A community or church sports program, such as an adult softball league or YMCA volleyball league;

- An interscholastic or intramural after-school league at the junior high school or high school levels;
- A part of the league system at a local bowling alley;
- An independent league sponsored by businesses or civic groups;
- A program in cooperation with a local recreation and park association.

Athletes with mental retardation who participate in Unified Sports may or may not be involved in the local Special Olympics programs. Athletes without mental retardation can be recruited from schools, corporations, civic groups or other community organizations. These athletes must be similar in age and skill level to the athletes with mental retardation who participate in the program.

Unified Sports teams are coached by volunteer coaches who may attend a Special Olympics Coaches Training School in the appropriate sport. Teams may participate in Unified Sports divisions at Special Olympics Area, Chapter and International Games.

MATP

The Motor Activities Training Program (MATP) provides comprehensive motor activity and recreation training for people with severe handicaps, emphasizing training and participation rather than competition. The MATP has been developed with the cooperation of physical educators, physical therapists, and recreation therapists and has been field-tested in the United States and several other countries. The MATP is part of the commitment by Special Olympics to offer sports training opportunities to all individuals with mental retardation.

The MATP trains participants in motor-based recreation activities and enables them to take part in a program which is appropriate to the age and ability of each individual. After a training period of at least eight weeks, participants may take part in a Special Olympics Training Day, giving each participant a chance to demonstrate his or her "personal best" in an activity and to be recognized for this accomplishment. The skills learned through the MATP also enable people with severe handicaps to participate in community recreational activities with their non-handicapped peers.

While the goal of the MATP is not necessarily to prepare persons with severe handicaps to participate in sports, many MATP participants will gain the skills required to compete in certain Special Olympics sports events.

The MATP trains participants in seven basic motor skills designed to relate to specific sports (examples below). The skills also complement training by educators and therapists in daily living skills. The MATP trains participants in:

- Mobility-Gymnastics
- Dexterity-Athletics
- Striking-Softball
- Kicking-Football (Soccer)
- Manual Wheelchair-Athletics
- Electric Wheelchair-Athletics
- Aquatics-Aquatics

The MATP can be implemented through schools, group homes, residential facilities and other community-based settings. While trainers may have previous experience in physical therapy, training for volunteers is available through Special Olympics Motor Activities Training Schools conducted by local Special Olympics programs.

Athletes for Outreach

In 1987, Special Olympics launched an important outreach campaign called "Join the World of Winners," whereby twice as many individuals with mental retardation would be provided Special Olympics sports training and competition within the next four years.

Early in 1988, a Colorado Special Olympics athlete named Greg Mark decided that he should be part of the outreach campaign. He recruited 30 of his friends—adults who had stopped competing in Special Olympics—to become involved again. Mark's action inspired a program called **Athletes for Outreach**, through which Special Olympics athletes are trained to give formal presentations to peers and potential athletes, civic, sports and church groups, school and community administrators, and families. The purpose of each presentation is to recruit new Special Olympics athletes and the volunteers needed to expand programs.

Training consists of three-day workshops conducted by Special Olympics staff and experts in public speaking. The workshop requires each athlete to give a five-minute presentation, after which he/she is critiqued by peers and trainers.

Each **Athlete for Outreach** is then asked to give five presentations per year, to report on the presentations and their results, and to recruit, by means of a registration form, new athletes both during the presentations and at every opportunity.

The first group of fifteen athletes from eleven states was trained in May, 1988. Since then, each one of the **Athletes for Outreach** has made a significant contribution to public awareness of Special Olympics in their communities and states across the country.

Special Olympics Athletes for Outreach have:

- Given two presentations at the National Down Syndrome Congress;
- Spoken at State Directors of Special Education and Superintendents of Education meetings;
- Been the keynote speaker at a Special Olympics Chapter Leadership conference and spoken at the Special Olympics National Conference and National Torch Run Conference;
- Given presentations to college and university classes;
- Appeared in a televion commercial for Special Olympics;
- Appeared in a nationally televised Special Olympics Christmas Special;
- Been the keynote speaker at the National PTA Convention;
- Delivered a speech at the Opening Ceremonies of the 1989 Winter International Games.

How to Become Involved in Special Olympics

Special Olympics is administered almost entirely by volunteers of all ages and from all backgrounds. Volunteers are students, senior citizens, members of civic and fraternal groups, amateur and professional athletes, sports officials and coaches, teachers, parents, business people, and others representing virtually all sectors of the community.

There is an opportunity and a place for anyone who wishes to contribute volunteer effort. Some of the ways in which individuals can become involved are described in the categories below:

Sports Training

- Serve as certified Special Olympics coaches.
- Use specific sports expertise to help set up sports clinics or Special Olympics Training Schools.
- Organize, coach or play on Unified Sports teams. Train individuals with more severe handicaps through the Motor Activities Training Program.
- Help run Special Olympics sports camps.
- Obtain athletic equipment or uniforms for Special Olympics athletes or teams.

Competitions

- Serve as certified officials or Games Directors.

- Serve as timers, scorers or team managers at Special Olympics Games.
- Conduct clinics or demonstrations in a new sport.
- Assist with registration, computer input or awards processing.
- Serve as drivers or food service workers at Special Olympics Games.
- Organize recreational and social events for athletes, such as Olympic Town, dances or entertainment.

Schools

- Include Special Olympics sports training programs in the adapted physical education curriculum or after-school sports program, utilizing the Special Olympics Sports Skills Program Guides.
- Open school athletic facilities to Special Olympics events.
- Organize members of school sports teams to become certified Special Olympics coaches.
- Start Special Olympics Unified Sports teams or Sports Partnerships as part of the existing extracurricular sports program.
- Start Special Olympics Partners Clubs.
- Conduct Special Olympics sports competitions or demonstrations during regular sports events.

• Provide volunteer support at Special Olympics Games.

Fund-raising

• Make financial or in-kind donations as an individual or business.
• Support the Law Enforcement Torch Run for Special Olympics through corporate sponsorship or the Adopt-A-Cop program.
• Conduct fund-raising campaigns in schools or through a civic group, church or other organization.
• Name Special Olympics as the beneficiary of a life insurance policy, will or employee payroll.

Professional

• Help establish a Special Olympics program in workplaces employing individuals with mental retardation.
• Provide medical support including free physical examinations and X-rays.
• Provide pro-bono legal or accounting services.
• Contribute computer skills to help manage Special Olympics' computer needs.
• Sponsor a Special Olympics team.
• Organize a Unified Sports team combining employees with Special Olympics athletes.

- Make in-kind donations of goods or services to Special Olympics.
- Donate office supplies and equipment to the local Special Olympics program.

Public Awareness

- Write articles about Special Olympics athletes, families and coaches.
- Volunteer copywriting, photography, or public relations skills to local, state or national Special Olympics program.
- Take part in a telephone campaign to inform people about Special Olympics.
- Man the media center or serve as a press escort at a Special Olympics event.
- Join a Special Olympics Speakers Bureau.
- Help train Special Olympics athletes to give presentations through the Athletes for Outreach program.

Administrative

- Serve on Chapter/National Program Boards of Directors, or Area Committees.
- Help special education teachers or Special Olympics coaches prepare registration and medical forms.
- Contribute typing, filing and computer skills as a volunteer in a Special Olympics office.

• Help with mass mailing projects.
• Distribute flyers and posters for Special Olympics events.

Civic Groups

• Provide volunteer support for a Special Olympics program or event.
• Adopt a local Special Olympics program or team.
• Organize a Unified Sports team combining members with Special Olympics athletes.
• Encourage members to volunteer their professional services for a Special Olympics program. Friends to Special Olympics Athletes
• Serve as a "hugger," escort or cheerleader at Special Olympics Games.
• Take part in recreational or social outings such as a hike or a picnic with Special Olympics athletes.
• Help transport athletes to and from practice and competitions.
• Work as a volunteer at a group home or institution.

For more information contact:
SPECIAL OLYMPICS INTERNATIONAL
HEADQUARTERS
1350 New York Avenue, N.W. – Suite 500
Washington, D.C. 20005
(202) 628-3630

Accredited Special Olympics Programs Around the World — By Region:

Africa and the Middle East

Botswana	Israel	Senegal
Burkina Faso	Jordan	The Seychelles
Cote d'Ivoire	Kenya	Sierra Leone
Egypt	Lebanon	Tanzania
The Gambia	Nigeria	Togo
Ghana	Reunion	Zambia
Guinea	Saudi Arabia	Zimbabwe

Asia/Pacific

Australia	Japan	People's Republic
Bangladesh	Korea	of China
Chinese Taipei	Macau	Philippines
Hong Kong	Nepal	Singapore
India	New Zealand	Thailand
Indonesia	Pakistan	

The Caribbean

Antigua	Dominica	St. Kitts & Nevis
Bahamas	Grenada	St. Lucia
Barbados	Guadeloupe	St. Vincent &
Belize	Guyana	and Grenadines
Bermuda	Jamaica	Suriname
Cayman Islands	Martinique	Trinidad & Tobago
Curacao		

Europe

Austria	Hungary	Poland
Belgium	Iceland	Portugal
Cyprus	Ireland	San Marino
Czechoslovakia	Italy	Spain
Denmark	Latvia	Switzerland
Estonia	Lithuania	Turkey
France	Luxembourg	United Kingdom

Gibraltar
Greece

Monaco
Norway

U.S.S.R.
Yugoslavia

Latin America

Argentina
Bolivia
Brazil
Chile
Colombia
Costa Rica
Cuba

Dominican Republic
Ecuador
El Salvador
Guatemala
Honduras
Mexico
Nicaragua

Panama
Paraguay
Peru
Puerto Rico
Uruguay
Venezuela

North America

Canada

United States
of America

Sites and Dates of The International Special Olympics Games:

Summer

lst	Chicago IL (Soldier Field)	July 19-20, 1968
2nd	Chicago IL (Soldier Field)	Aug 13-15, 1970
3rd	Los Angeles CA (U.C.L.A.)	Aug 13-18, 1972
4th	Mt. Pleasant MI (Central Michigan U.)	Aug 7-11, 1975
5th	Brockport NY (State U. of N.Y.)	Aug 8-13, 1979
6th	Baton Rouge LA (Louisiana State U.)	July 12-18, 1983
7th	South Bend IN (Notre Dame U.)	July 31-Aug. 8, 1987
8th	Minneapolis/St. Paul MN (Multiple locations)	July 19-27, 1991

Winter

1st	Steamboat Springs CO	Feb 5-11, 1977
2nd	Village of Smuggler's Notch and Stowe VT	Mar 8–13, 1981
3rd	Park City UT	Mar 24-29, 1985
4th	Reno NV and Lake Tahoe CA	Apr 1-8, 1989

A Special Thanks

The publishers wish to extend their appreciation to Larry Barnett for his tremendous contribution to the production of this book and to those at Special Olympics International who were a helpful resource in providing facts and background on Special Olympics and the many programs which are part of the organization.

About the Author

Mary Francess Froese is a free-lance writer who has contributed articles to several magazines and inspirational books. Currently, she is secretary to a San Diego County district supervisor and a regular newspaper reporter and special features writer. Mary and her husband, Allen, reside in Vista, California. They have two grown sons, Scott and Joel. *Heroes of a Special Kind* is Mary's first book.